Korean **Reading**
Made Simple

GO! Billy Korean

Korean Reading Made Simple
Volume 1, Edition 1

Written by: Billy Go
Artwork and editing by: Sohyun Sohn
Cover design by: Joel Tersigni
Cover artwork by: Heejin Park
Published by: GO! Billy Korean

Printed by Amazon Kindle Direct Publishing (KDP)
Available from Amazon.com and other retail outlets

ISBN: 9781675282779

TABLE OF CONTENTS

Preface

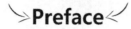

Welcome back! Or if you're seeing me for the first time, 안녕! I'm Billy, and I'm here to help you along your Korean language journey! I'm so glad to see that you're seeking out more resources (such as this one, and hopefully others) to continue studying and practicing the language. Did you know that the majority of Korean learners give up in the very early stages, such as while learning the alphabet or basic grammar? There are many reasons that happens, and I won't judge those who do – especially because I know myself how difficult learning Korean can be at times. The fact that you've conquered the basics and are now working hard to pass through the intermediate (or advanced) level is something that you can and should feel proud of. Always remember the reasons why you're learning Korean, and use that to help motivate yourself to keep going.

Learning Korean is a lot like trying to level up in a video game – it's easy in the beginning, then gets progressively harder. When you first started learning it might have only taken a few hours or days to memorize 한글 and some useful phrases. Perhaps you were able to even put together a complete simple sentence after a few weeks of studying. Everything was moving so quickly. However, past the beginning stages things can feel slower; you start to need more and more time and effort to notice yourself improving and to reach that next level. But in order to push past those barriers it will not only require more studying, but also more exposure to the language. This exposure includes speaking, writing, listening, and *reading* – each are helpful and important.

When it comes to reading, there's a lot more out there than just Korean novels. In this book alone you'll explore newspaper articles, journal entries, emails, poems, folk tales, social media posts, and even comics. The more variety you have, the better. Through the resources in this book you'll not only be able to improve your general reading comprehension, but you'll also be increasing your exposure to a wider variety of written content (including ones you may not have tried yet). And finally, it's my hope that you'll be able to gain a greater appreciation for written materials in the Korean language.

Good luck in your studies!

What You Can Expect

It can be difficult jumping straight into native-level materials, whether you're intermediate or even advanced. This book is meant to be a bridge to allow learners to explore completely natural, real-life reading resources along with explanations, translations, and definitions. Imagine trying to read something that was written for a native Korean speaker (not simplified for a beginner) and having a personal tutor right by your side to walk you through it – that's this book.

Preface

Each resource comes together with translations, definitions, and explanations for both its vocabulary and grammar forms – all tailored specifically to a Korean learner (that's you). This will help any learner with basic grammar and vocabulary under their belt (and a dictionary) to dive into the deep end and experience true and natural reading materials in Korean. In order to save space, grammar and vocabulary will be defined and explained briefly within the context of the resource; concepts will be covered enough to be able to fully comprehend each resource.

English translations will be more *literal* than natural – this is to help you understand the Korean content more easily. Natural translations will also be provided occasionally. The Korean language uses different phrases and grammar than English – even the way Koreans think when speaking and writing is unique – and I wanted to preserve that in the English translations as much as possible.

This book should not be used as a standard textbook if you're still moving through the beginner level; instead I recommend my "Korean Made Simple" textbook series which goes from the very beginning of the language up to the intermediate level (or you can use any textbook and resources you'd like). Before using this book you should first be able to have simple, basic Korean conversations (even if very slowly); this typically happens around the lower intermediate level.

Tips for Using This Book

Keep a Korean dictionary handy while using this book. While most vocabulary words in this book will be defined, simpler and more common words or grammar forms will not be. Also I recommend that you refer to the glossary section whenever you find a word or grammar form that you're not familiar with – the number next to each entry is the number of the resource it first appears in (listed in the Table of Contents).

Words and grammar defined in a previous chapter of this book will not be defined again in later chapters. Because of this, I recommend moving through these resources in the order they're given without skipping any (but don't let me tell you what to do).

Try not to rush. It'd be much better to read through the resources and explanations slowly so that you can understand them. I recommend first reading each resource on your own before looking at any of the translations or explanations. Or if you're already at a higher level, try reading the resource on its own two or three times, and then only relying on the explanations or definitions when you get stuck.

Preface

The Plain Form

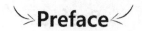

You'll often find the Plain Form used in many written resources. The Plain Form is especially common in newspaper articles, essays, journals, and short stories. It's used whenever there's no specific intended audience.

The Plain Form includes using 나 instead of 저 (when spoken, 나 is typically only used in casual speech) as well as ending verbs with 다 when conjugating. Here's a (very) quick overview of how to conjugate the Plain Form. For the present tense, attach ㄴ다 to a verb stem that ends in a vowel, or attach 는다 to a verb stem that ends in a consonant. Verb stems ending with ㄹ will remove the ㄹ and attach ㄴ다.

가다 → 가 + ㄴ다 → **간다**
먹다 → 먹 + 는다 → **먹는다**
살다 → 살 – ㄹ → 사 + ㄴ다 → **산다**

For the past tense, first conjugate the verb as usual (using the 요 form), cut off any syllable after the ㅆ ending, and then attach 다. However, 이다 ("to be") becomes 이었다 after a consonant or 였다 after a vowel. 아니다 ("to not be") simply becomes 아니었다.

가다 → 갔어요 → 갔 + 다 → **갔다**
먹다 → 먹었어요 → 먹었 + 다 → **먹었다**
있다 → 있었어요 → 있었 + 다 → **있었다**
이다 → 이었어요 or 였어요 → 이었 or 였 + 다 → **이었다** or **였다**
아니다 → 아니었어요 → 아니었 + 다 → **아니었다**

Additional Questions?

Feel free to contact me 24/7 with any questions you have and I'll try to get back to you (but give me a day or so to check my email). I love helping people like you to learn Korean, and appreciate your support through purchasing this book. You can find my contact information in the "About the Author" section at the back of this book.

해남 김 토끼 가족 1화

해남 김 토끼 가족 1 화
"The Haenam Kim Rabbit Family, Episode 1"

해남 is a county in southwestern Korea known for its seafood and 김 – dried seaweed or laver. This is to suggest the black spots on the rabbits' ears might be actual 김. In addition, 해남 김 could also mean a 김 ("Kim") family whose genealogy is from 해남.

김 = "dried seaweed," "(dried) laver"
화 = episode counter

여보, 나 다녀올게요.
"Honey, I'll be off now."

여보 can be used to refer to one's husband or wife – similarly to saying "honey" or "sweetheart" – although it's not commonly used between younger married couples.

다녀올게(요) is a combination of 다니다 meaning "to attend (school)" or "to commute (to work)" and 오다 meaning "to come." It's a phrase used literally to mean that you'll "go (to work or school) and come back" the same day. When announcing that you're leaving it's common to use 다녀오다 or just 갔다 오다 ("to go and come") – simply saying 갈게(요) would be like announcing that you're leaving without reassuring the listener that you have plans to return yet.

여보 = "honey," "sweetheart"
다녀오다 = "to go and come back"

잠깐만요, 당신 넥타이요.
"Hold on, your tie."

당신 is a *literal* translation for "you," but is not commonly used between younger married couples – some couples may use it to refer to each other like "darling."

당신 = "darling," "you"
넥타이 = "(neck)tie"

해남 김 토끼 가족 1화

아차, 또 깜빡했네. 고마워요. 그럼 다녀올게요.

"Oh my, I forgot again. Thanks. Well then, I'll be going."

아차 is an expression used when you suddenly realize that you've made a mistake.

깜빡하다 is used when you've only momentarily forgotten about something that you otherwise know.

아차! = "Oh my!," "Darn it!," "My goodness!"
깜빡하다 = "to forget (momentarily)"

잠깐만요!

"Wait!"

컴퓨터 가지고 가야죠.

"You need to bring your computer."

가야죠 is a spoken contraction of 가야 하죠. Literally, the whole sentence 컴퓨터 가지고 가야죠 means "You need to bring your computer," but a more natural translation of the ~야죠 form (also ~야지 in casual speech) might be as a *command* – "Bring your computer!" In this way it's similar to saying, "Bring your computer, okay?"

이런, 내 정신 좀 봐.

"Oh no, how could I have forgotten that."

내 정신 좀 봐 literally means "look at my mind/consciousness," and is for when you've forgotten about something or forgotten to do something.

이런 = "darn," "dang it," "oh no"
정신 = "mind," "consciousness"
내 정신 좀 봐. = "I can't believe I've forgotten that."

큰일 날 뻔했네. 어떻게 이걸 놓고 가려고 했지. 그럼 다녀올게요.

"That was close. How could I have forgotten this? Well then, I'll be going."

놓고 가다 literally means "to leave and go," and is used when forgetting to *take* something with you. 놓고 오다 has the same meaning for *bringing*.

뻔하다 is attached after verb stems (followed by 을 after a consonant or ㄹ after a vowel) and means that someone "almost" or "nearly" did something, but didn't.

큰일 = "problem," "trouble" (literally, "big issue")

큰일(이) 나다 = "to be a big problem," "to get into trouble"

~(을/ㄹ) 뻔하다 = "to almost (do)," "to nearly (do)"

놓고 가다 = "to forget to take," "to leave (something) and go"

놓고 오다 = "to forget to bring," "to leave (something) and come"

잠깐만요!

"Wait!"

당신 도시락 가져가세요.

"Bring your lunch box."

도시락 = "lunch box," "prepared (box) lunch"

해남 김 토끼 가족 2화

해남 김 토끼 가족 2 화
"The Haenam Kim Rabbit Family, Episode 2"

여보, 나 가요. 문 잘 잠궈요.
"Honey, I'm going. Lock the door."

잠그다 means "to lock" or "to fasten" something, such as a room in a house or a cabinet. Its proper conjugation is 잠가(요) in the present tense, or 잠갔어(요) in the past tense; however, it's commonly conjugated *incorrectly* as 잠궈(요) and 잠궜어(요).

While 잘 literally means "well," it's being used in the sentence 문 잘 잠궈요 (잠가요) to mean "do a good job of locking up." You can also think of 잘 here as meaning "make sure to" lock up, or even "don't forget to" lock up.

잠그다 = "to lock"

잘 다녀오세요.
"Goodbye."

잘 다녀오세요 – or a variation such as 잘 다녀와(요) – can be said to someone who is leaving to school or work and will be returning later the same day. In this way, it's similar to saying "travel safely (to work or school)" or even just "see you later."

드디어 혼자 남았네. 변신해야겠다.
"I'm finally alone. I need to transform."

혼자 남다 literally means "to be left alone," but it doesn't mean that nothing is bothering you anymore – rather, it means that you're all alone after everyone else has left.

해야겠다 is a shorter and more casual version of 해야 하겠다, meaning "(I) need to." Here, the rabbit is talking about transforming herself into a superhero.

해남 김 토끼 가족 2화

드디어 = "finally," "at last"
남다 = "to be left," "to remain"
변신(을) 하다 = "to transform," "to change"

가자!
"Let's go!"

악당들에게서 세상을 구하자!
"Let's save the world from the bad guys!"

악당 = "villain," "bad guy"
구하다 = "to rescue," "to save"
세상(을) 구하다 = "to save the world"

따르릉
"Ring!"

따르릉 is the sound that a phone, bell, or alarm makes when ringing. It can also be doubled as 따르릉 따르릉 ("Ring! Ring!").

따르릉 (따르릉) = "ring" (sound of telephone, bicycle bell, alarm clock)

따르릉
"Ring!"

전화다! 누구지? 시장님인가? 아니면 대통령?
"A phone call! Who is it? The mayor? Or the president?"

Note how 아니면 ("or") can be used at the start of a new sentence, and not only between two nouns ("this or that") like in English.

전화 = "phone call"
아니면 = "or"
시장님 = "(city) mayor"
대통령 = "president"

1 시간 뒤...
"After 1 hour..."

뒤 = "after," "behind"

해남 김 토끼 가족 2화

호호호, 정말? 어머 어머!

"Oh, really? Oh my!"

어머 (어머) is an expression used most often by females to show surprise toward something unexpected, or to express shock.

어머 (어머)! = "Oh my!"

영희가 그랬다고? 아니야, 안 바빠. 계속 얘기해 봐.

"Yung-hee said that? No, I'm not busy. Keep talking."

그랬다고 is a combination of 그러다 (a shortened version of 그렇게 말하다 meaning "to say so") in the past tense combined with the quoting ending ~고 (here meaning "she said..."). Together, 영희가 그랬다고 literally means "(someone) says that Yung-hee said that?" 그러다 can also be used to mean "to do that."

그러다 = "to say so," "to do so"

해남 김 토끼 가족 3화

해남 김 토끼 가족 3 화

"The Haenam Kim Rabbit Family, Episode 3"

이번 역은 강남, 강남역입니다. 내리실 문은 오른쪽입니다.

"This station is Gangnam, Gangnam Station. The doors to get off are on the right side."

내리실 문 comes from the honorific form of 내리다 – 내리시다 – which means "to get off (a vehicle)" or "to disembark." Here it's used in the future tense as an adjective with 문 ("door") – literally, "door(s) that (you) will disembark (through)."

오른쪽 = "right (side)"

내리다 = "to get off (a vehicle)," "to disembark"

드르렁

Snoring loudly.

드르렁 (드르렁) = (sound of snoring)

아이고, 배추 가격이 또 올랐네.

"Oh my, the cabbage price went up again."

오르다 is an intransitive verb (it does not use an object) that means something rises, and here is used to talk about the price of cabbage going up. To "raise" the price of cabbage as a transitive verb (with an object), use 올리다 instead.

배추 = "cabbage"

오르다 = "to go up," "to rise," "to increase"

올리다 = "to raise," "to increase"

이번 역은 사당, 사당역입니다. 내리실 문은 왼쪽입니다.

"This station is Sadang, Sadang Station. The doors to get off are on your left side."

왼쪽 = "left (side)"

나도 사랑해, 엄마.

"I love you too, mom."

해남 김 토끼 가족 3화

으악! 깜빡 잠들었다. 여기가 어디야? 사당? 이런.
"Ugh! I suddenly fell asleep! Where am I? Sadang? Dang it."

으악 is an expression or sound used either to show disgust, or suddenly being surprised.

깜빡 is an adverb that means "with a flash," and it's used to show that something happens suddenly while your mind is blank or without you being aware.

으악 = "Ugh!," "Ah!" (surprise)
깜빡 = "with a flash"
깜빡 잠(이) 들다 = "to fall asleep (without being aware of it)"

안녕하세요.
"Hello."

안녕하세요. 강남역이요. 빨리 가주세요.
"Hello. Gangnam Station. Please go quickly."

Simply ending the sentence with 강남역 ("Gangnam Station") would sound a bit too informal. When ending a sentence with a noun, add 이요 after a consonant or 요 after a vowel when you need to be more polite.

네, 알겠습니다.
"Okay, I got it."

슝!
Whoosh!

슝 = "whoosh" (sound of wind, flying)

파워토끼입니다. 도착시간 3 분 남았습니다.
"This is Power Rabbit. 3 minutes left till arrival."

Usually when Sino-Korean words are combined into compound nouns (when two words that have 한자 origins become one single word), they do so without a space. 도착 ("arrival") and 시간 ("time") combine as one word to form 도착시간 ("arrival time").

남다 can be used in the past tense to show that something remains or is left over. Alternatively, you could also use 남아 있다 to show that something is *right now* in the state of being remaining or left over. Both 3 분 남았습니다 and 3 분 남아 있습니다 would be correct.

도착시간 = "arrival time"

해남 김 토끼 가족 3화

어? 파워토끼다!

"Huh? It's Power Rabbit!"

우와, 하늘을 나네. 부럽다. 아침에 출근할 때 얼마나 좋을까....

"Wow, she's flying in the sky. I'm jealous. That must be so great for going to work in the morning."

날다 means "to fly," but to say that you fly in the sky use 하늘 with the Object Marker (을/를). You could also add the adverb 높이 ("high") as 하늘(을) 높이 날다 to mean "to fly high in the sky."

얼마나 means "how much," but it can also be used with descriptive verbs and the ~까(요) ending ("could," "would") to mean simply "how" – 얼마나 좋을까 literally means "How good would it be?"

날다 = "to fly"
하늘(을) 날다 = "to fly in the sky"
출근(을) 하다 = "to (leave to) go to work"
얼마나 = "how (much)," "how"

친구와 함께 고른 선물

친구와 함께 고른 선물

다음 주는 어머니의 생신이다. 어머니의 선물로 무엇이 좋을까 고민하다가 요즘 연락을 많이 하고 지내는 친구의 도움을 받아 선물을 골라보기로 했다. 수업이 끝나고 집에 들러서 가방을 바꿔서 가는 것이 좋다고 생각해서 오후 5시에 친구와 만나기로 했는데, 버스 정류장까지 걸어가다가 갑자기 비가 오는 바람에 다시 집에 돌아갈 수밖에 없었다. 시간이 부족해서 겨우 옷만 갈아입고 나갔는데도 약속시간에 30분이나 늦어서 친구에게 너무 미안했지만 불행인지 다행인지 친구는 나보다 15분이나 더 늦게 도착했다. 비가 많이 와서 여러 곳을 둘러보지 못하고 처음 들어간 화장품 가게에서 1시간 동안 신중하게 선물을 골랐다. 친구와 아르바이트생 누나들의 도움으로 최종적으로 립스틱을 골랐는데 누나들이 1시간 동안 직접 이것저것 발라보고 지워보면서 고르는 나와 내 친구가 너무 귀엽다며 포장까지 예쁘게 해주셨다. 비가 와서 그런지 떡볶이와 어묵이 생각나서 친구와 함께 저녁으로 먹었는데, 내가 산다고 하니 가게에 있는 어묵을 다 먹을 기세더라. 둘이 합쳐서 어묵 꼬치를 30개는 먹은 것 같다. 당분간 어묵 생각은 나지 않을 것 같다. 어머니께 드릴 선물이 작아 보이니 예쁜 손 편지도 써서 드리면 좋을 것 같은데, 마땅한 편지지가 있을지 모르겠다. 자기 전에 청소도 좀 할 겸 책상 서랍에 있는 것들을 다 꺼내봐야지. 어머니께서 마음에 들어 하시면 좋겠다.

친구와 함께 고른 선물

친구와 함께 고른 선물

"A present I chose together with a friend."

~(와/과) 함께 = "together with..."

고르다 = "to choose"

다음 주는 어머니의 생신이다.

"Next week is my mother's birthday."

어머니 ("mother") is the more polite-sounding and standard version of 엄마 ("mom"). Also, since the journal doesn't mention a different mother, we can assume the writer is talking about their own.

When talking about someone's birthday whom you would speak politely about, you can use 생신 ("birthday") instead of 생일 ("birthday") to show more respect. Like other honorific nouns, 생신 should only be used when talking about someone else's birthday, and not your own.

생신 = "birthday" (honorific)

어머니의 선물로 무엇이 좋을까 고민하다가 요즘 연락을 많이 하고 지내는 친구의 도움을 받아 선물을 골라보기로 했다.

"While worrying about what would be good for my mother's gift, I decided to try choosing a gift with the help of a friend who I'm contacting a lot and getting along with lately."

무엇이 좋을까 is literally "what would be good." The ~(을/ㄹ)까 ending (meaning "would" or "shall") is being used here together with the verb 고민(을) 하다 to mean "to worry what would be good." Note that 고민(을) 하다 is not used to show a strong concern or worry – if you're worried about something serious, use 걱정(을) 하다 ("to worry," "to concern") instead. 고민(을) 하다 can be used for small concerns or worries, such as worrying (or even just "wondering") what you should wear for a date, or what to eat for dinner.

지내다 is used to mean that you "get along" with someone, so 연락을 많이 하고 지내는 친구 means "a friend who I'm contacting a lot and getting along (or associating) with."

도움을 받아 has the same meaning as 도움을 받아서, but removing 서 like this is only common in writing. The ~서 ending can be used to mean that the first action (getting the friend's help) is how the second action was able to happen (choosing a gift). In this way, you can also think of 친구의 도움을 받아(서) as meaning "*through* getting my friend's help...."

골라보기로 했다 uses the ending ~기로 하다 attached to the verb stem (here, 골라보다 meaning "to try choosing"); this ending means "to decide to do" and is often used in the past tense to mean that you've already chosen or decided to do something. You might also see this form as ~기로 결정(을) 하다.

친구와 함께 고른 선물

고민(을) 하다 = "to be concerned," "to (slightly) worry"
걱정(을) 하다 = "to worry," "to concern"
지내다 = "to associate with," "to get along with"
도움(을) 받다 = "to get/receive help"
~기로 하다 = "to decide to do..."
결정(을) 하다 = "to decide"

수업이 끝나고 집에 들러서 가방을 바꿔서 가는 것이 좋다고 생각해서 오후 5 시에 친구와 만나기로 했는데...

"After class finishes, I thought it would be good to stop by at home and change my bag and go, so at 5 o'clock PM I decided to meet a friend, but..."

The ~고 ending can be used to mean "and" as well as show that one action happens after another – a good way to translate this form can also be "and then." So 끝나고 can translate as either "ends and then" or "after ending."

The verb 들르다 conjugates as 들러 (or 들러요 in the 요 form). Note that this is also commonly conjugated *incorrectly* as 들려.

The ~서 ending is being used here to show that two actions are directly connected with each other, and that one action happens immediately following another. Here, the second action (going) is happening immediately after the first action (changing their bag) – you can think of 들러서 가방을 바꿔서 가는 [...] as meaning "stop by home and then (immediately) change my bag and then (immediately) go."

You can express thoughts with 생각(을) 하다 meaning "to think" and the Plain Form. 좋다고 생각하다 would therefore translate as "to think that it's good." Making suggestions using an action verb together with the ~는 ending and 것 – such as in the example, 가는 것 – is one way to express your opinion of an action (whether that action *would* be a certain way). Saying 가는 것이 좋아요 could translate as "it's good if you would go," and 공부하는 것이 제일 나아요 could translate as "it would be (most) preferable if you would study."

The ~데 ending is being used here to show contrast between two sentences – much in the same way as using "and" (the ~고 ending) or "but" (the ~지만 ending). However, this contrast is softer than "but" and not as strong as "and," so it's useful as a simple way to connect sentences or show contrast.

수업 = "class," "lesson" (taught by a teacher)
들르다 = "to stop by"

버스 정류장까지 걸어가다가 갑자기 비가 오는 바람에 다시 집에 돌아갈 수밖에 없었다.

"Since it suddenly rained while walking to the bus stop I (unfortunately) had no choice but to go back home again."

까지 is being used here to show that some movement (걸어가다) happens "up until" a *location*. You can think of it as meaning "all the way to," but more naturally it can just translate as "to."

친구와 함께 고른 선물

바람에 is used when explaining the reason for something bad that has happened. Because of this, it can add the meaning of "unfortunately." It's attached after an action verb conjugated to an adjective in the present tense; for example, 가다 would become 가는, and 먹다 would become 먹는. Note that the rest of the sentence (what it is that happened) after 바람에 will always end in the past tense.

When attached directly to a verb stem, ~(을/ㄹ) 수밖에 없다 means that "there's nothing one can do except" do whatever verb it's used with. For example, 걱정할 수밖에 없어요 could translate as "There's nothing I can do but worry." Another way to translate this grammar form is "to have no choice but to do."

까지 = "(up) until," "(all the way) to (a location)"
걸어가다 = "to walk (to somewhere)"
바람에 = "due to (something negative)"
~(을/ㄹ) 수밖에 없다 = "nothing one can do but"

시간이 부족해서 겨우 옷만 갈아입고 나갔는데도 약속시간에 30 분이나 늦어서...

"There's not enough time, so even though I just barely only changed my clothes and went out I was late as much as 30 minutes for my meeting (time), so..."

부족하다 is used after a noun to mean that noun is lacking, or that there's not enough of it. With 시간, it means that there's not enough time.

겨우 means that you're only *barely* doing something – and with difficulty. Therefore, 겨우 옷만 갈아입고 could translate as "barely change only (my) clothes and then...."

갈아입다 comes from the combination of 갈다 ("replace" or "change") and 입다 ("to wear"). Note that depending on the type of clothing you're wearing, a different verb for "to wear" may be used. For example, changing shoes would be 갈아 신다, since shoes are worn with 신다 ("to wear"). You can also "transfer" (change how you're riding somewhere) using 갈아타다 (from 갈다 and 타다), such as going from one subway line to another.

The ~데 ending when combined with the particle 도 ("also," "even," "too") can translate as "even though." 나갔는데도 could therefore translate as "even though I went out."

약속 ("promise," "appointment") is also commonly used to refer to any sort of meeting that you scheduled with someone (even a friend). 약속시간, although literally "appointment time," can also mean simply "the time you agreed to meet someone."

Attaching (이)나 to a noun gives it the meaning of "or something," but when attached to a time has the meaning of "no less than" or "as much/long as."

친구와 함께 고른 선물

To say what it is that you're late to – using 늦다 ("to be late") – use the particle 에. 모임에 늦다 would therefore mean "to be late to a meeting."

부족하다 = "to be insufficient," "to be lacking"
겨우 = "(just) barely"
갈아입다 = "to change (clothing)"
~데도 = "even though"
약속시간 = "appointment/meeting time"
~(이)나 = "or something," "no less than," "as much/long as," "as many as," "about"
~에 늦다 = "to be late to"

친구에게 너무 미안했지만 불행인지 다행인지 친구는 나보다 15 분이나 더 늦게 도착했다.

"I felt so sorry to my friend, but maybe it was misfortune or luck (that) my friend arrived no less than 15 minutes later than me."

미안하다 means "to be sorry," but is also used to mean that you *feel* sorry about something. Use 에게 (or 한테) to show who it is you feel sorry toward.

불행인지 다행인지 uses the verb 이다 ("to be"), and here can translate as "whether it is... or...." The ~지 ending attached to a verb is what carries the meaning of "whether (or not)."

Since 늦게 도착하다 means "to arrive late," 더 늦게 도착하다 means "to arrive later." Literally, 더 늦게 means "more late."

불행 = "misfortune"
다행 = "good fortune," "luck"
~지... ~지 = "whether (or not)"

비가 많이 와서 여러 곳을 둘러보지 못하고 처음 들어간 화장품 가게에서 1 시간 동안 신중하게 선물을 골랐다.

"It rained a lot so we couldn't look around many places, and at the first cosmetics store we entered we carefully chose a gift for 1 hour."

The ending ~지 못하다 means that you're unable to do something, so 둘러보지 못하다 means you're unable to have a look around.

여러 means "a number of" or "several," but since it's being used in a negative sentence – 둘러보지 못하고 – a better translation here could be "we couldn't have a look around many (various) places."

신중하다 means "to be cautious" or "to be careful," but a more natural translation for 신중하게 선물을 골랐다 could be something like "we *took our time* choosing a present." In this way, 신중하게 ("cautiously," "carefully") is being used here to mean "without rushing" or "not hastily."

여러 = "a number of," "several," "many"
여러 곳 = "a number of places," "several places"
둘러보다 = "to (have a) look around," "to browse"
~지 못하다 = "unable to (do)," "can't (do)"
들어가다 = "to enter (in)"
화장품 = "cosmetics"
신중하다 = "to be cautious," "to be careful"

친구와 아르바이트생 누나들의 도움으로 최종적으로 립스틱을 골랐는데...

"With the help of my friend, and the (older female) employees (at the store), we finally chose a lipstick, but..."

아르바이트생 is a combination of 아르바이트 meaning "part-time job" (also shortened to 알바) and the Hanja (Chinese character) word 생 meaning "student." Note that 생 and most other single-syllable Hanja words cannot be used on their own (학생 is the normal word for "student"), but must be combined with another word to have this meaning. Together it means "a student who's working a part-time job," and is used to refer to a college student who works while going to school. The word 누나 ("an older female friend," "older sister") is being used here to simply mean "an older female," and not to mean that she is an actual friend or sibling.

도움으로 is a combination of 도움 ("help") and (으)로, here being used to mean "by means of" or "with."

최종 by itself means "final" or "last," but combined with the Hanja word 적 changes the meaning to "finally" or "lastly." Words ending with 적 are often used with the particle (으)로 as adverbs to show the way in which something is done – here, 최종적으로 can mean "finally..." or "in the end...." Alternatively, words ending in 적 are also commonly used with 이다 (conjugated to 인) as adjectives – 최종적인 could mean "the final," "the last," or even "the definitive."

아르바이트 = "part-time job"
알바 = "part-time job"
아르바이트생 = "a student working a part-time job"
최종 = "final," "last"
최종적으로 = "finally," "lastly," "in the end"
최종적이다 = "to be the final," "to be the last," "to be the definitive"

누나들이 1 시간 동안 직접 이것저것 발라보고 지워보면서 고르는 나와 내 친구가 너무 귀엽다며...

"The female employees said that me and my friend who were choosing it (lipstick) were so cute, while we directly tried on and wiped off this and that for an hour."

Since this is a long sentence, let's break it down a bit. Here, 누나들이 are the female employees in the store, and what the employees are doing comes at the very end of the sentence – 나와 내 친구가 너무 귀엽다며. We'll talk about this part later, but it will help to break the sentence up in this way when understanding it.

직접 means "directly" or "personally," so here "me and my friend" are testing the lipstick directly by applying it on ourselves for an hour.

The ending ~(으)면서 means "while," and is only used when the person doing the action that comes before this form is the same as the person doing the action that comes after – so the person doing 지워보면서 ("while wiping off") must also be the same person who is 고르는 ("choosing").

The ~(으)며 ending can be used in the same way as ~(으)면서 to mean "while," but it can also be used to mean "and" (like the ~고 ending). For example, 영희 씨가 예쁘며 친절해요 would mean "Yung-hee is pretty and friendly." The ~(으)며 ending is more common in writing than in speaking.

귀엽다며 is a shortened version of the quoting form 귀엽다고 (말)하며, meaning "says that we are cute." Often the quoting ending ~다고 하다 is shortened to 다(고 하)다. Therefore, 있다고 하면서 can be shortened to 있다면서 or 있다며, 있다고 하네(요) can be shortened to 있다네(요), and 있다고 해(요) can be shortened to 있대(요).

직접 = "directly," "personally"
이것저것 = "this and that"
바르다 = "to apply," "to spread"
지우다 = "to wipe off," "to erase"
~(으)면서 = "while doing"
~(으)며 = "while," "and"

포장까지 예쁘게 해주셨다.

"And they even wrapped it up nicely for us."

Here, 까지 is being used to mean "even (as much as)," and is used to emphasize what someone went as far as to do. 포장까지 해주셨다 could also translate as "They even went as far as to wrap it up (for us)."

포장(을) 하다 = "to wrap up"
~까지 = "even (as much as)," "to go as far as to do"

비가 와서 그런지 떡볶이와 어묵이 생각나서 친구와 함께 저녁으로 먹었는데...

"Maybe because it rained I thought about spicy rice cakes and fish cake, so I ate that together with my friend for dinner, but..."

The ~서 ending can be used together with 그런지 (from 그렇다 meaning "to be so") to mean "whether because." This form is used as a way to guess the reason for something, and you can also think of it as meaning "maybe it's because of...."

떡볶이 is "spicy rice cakes," a common street food made with spicy sauce, along with usually fish cake (어묵), green onions, hard-boiled eggs, and even sometimes mozzarella cheese.

친구와 함께 고른 선물

생각(이) 나다 literally means "a thought comes to mind," and is used to mean "to think of" someone or something Here, it's being used to mean that you thought about 떡볶이 and 어묵, meaning that you remembered they existed.

저녁으로 means "for dinner," and the (으)로 particle can be used with any meal to mean "for." For example, you could ask someone what they want to eat for breakfast by asking 아침으로 뭐 먹을까요?

~(아/어/etc.) 서 그런지 = "whether it's because...," "maybe it's because..."
떡볶이 = "spicy rice cakes"
어묵 = "fish cake"
생각(이) 나다 = "to think of," "something comes to mind," "to be remembered"
저녁으로 = "for dinner"

내가 산다고 하니 가게에 있는 어묵을 다 먹을 기세더라.
"Because I said I'll buy it, I recall he looked like he was ready to eat all of the fish cake in the store."

The ~(으)니 ending used here has the same function and meaning as (으)니까 ("because"), but is more commonly used in writing than in speaking. Literally, 내가 산다고 (말)하니 means "because I said I'll buy it."

The form ~(을/ㄹ) 기세 is used together with the verb 이다 ("to be") to mean "to look/appear like someone will do" something, or more naturally just "to look ready to do" something. 기세 is a noun that means "vigor" or "one's spirits/enthusiasm," so this form literally means "to be in the spirits to do" something.

The ~더라 ending is used for describing something that you (the speaker) have personally experienced before. As such, you can think of it as meaning "I recall" or "I remember." This form has the same meaning as ~더라고(요), but is less polite since 더라 can't end with 요. 더라 also sounds slightly stronger than ~더라고(요) and therefore adds more emphasis on what you're saying that you've experienced.

~(으)니 = ~(으)니까
~(을/ㄹ) 기세이다 = "to look/appear like someone will do," "to be ready to do"
~더라 = (personally experienced, casual)
~더라고(요) = (personally experienced)

둘이 합쳐서 어묵 꼬치를 30 개는 먹은 것 같다.
"Together I think we ate 30 fish cake skewers."

둘이 is a combination of 둘 ("two") and the Subject Marker (이/가) to mean "two people" or "the two of us/them."

합쳐서 is from 합치다 ("to combine"), and together with 둘이 literally means "combining the two of us" or simply just "together (as one)."

친구와 함께 고른 선물

Using the Topic Marker (은/는) after the number 30 개 adds more emphasis to the large amount of fish cake skewers, because it changes the topic of conversation to that number. You can think of this part as meaning "As for 30 fish cake skewers (and not a single one less)... we ate them together."

둘이 = "two people," "the two of us/them"
합치다 = "to combine"
꼬치 = "(food on a) skewer"

당분간 어묵 생각은 나지 않을 것 같다.
"I don't think I'll think about fish cakes for some time."

당분간 can either mean "for some time," or it can mean "for the time being" depending on the context.

당분간 = "for some time," "for the time being"

어머니께 드릴 선물이 작아 보이니 예쁜 손 편지도 써서 드리면 좋을 것 같은데...
"Because the present that I'll give to my mom looks small, I think it'd be good if I write and give her a pretty handwritten letter too, but..."

께 is the honorific version of 에게 ("to" a person), and is commonly used in writing. Again, remember that honorifics (including particles) should only be used when talking about other people; 저께 ("to me") would be *incorrect* – use 저한테 or 저에게 instead.

드릴 is the future tense (adjective) form of the humble verb 드리다 ("to give"), and means "(that you) will give." Using this verb essentially *lowers* the speaker (yourself) to the person who they're giving something to (the mother). Because of this, it should not be used when talking about someone else giving something to you.

작아 보이다 is a combination of 작다 ("to be small") with 보이다 ("to be seen"). This grammar form using 보이다 is one way to express that something "looks" a certain way when used with descriptive verbs. For example, you could say that something looks delicious by using 맛있어 보이다, or that someone looks scared by using 무서워 보이다.

께 = "to" (honorific)
드리다 = "to give" (humble)
~(아/어/etc.) 보이다 = "to look (descriptive verb)"
손 편지 = "handwritten letter"

마땅한 편지지가 있을지 모르겠다.
"I don't know if I will have the right (kind of) stationary paper."

마땅하다 means "to be right" or "to be appropriate," but you can also think of it as "to be the right kind/type."

친구와 함께 고른 선물

편지지 is a combination of 편지 ("letter") and the Hanja word 지 ("paper") to mean "letter paper" or "stationary paper."

The grammar ending ~지 모르겠다 means "to not know whether/if…" and can be attached to a verb stem in the future tense (을/ㄹ), past tense (ㅆ는), or present tense (는 for action verbs or 은/ㄴ for descriptive verbs). For example, 가다 can be 갈지, 갔는지, or 가는지. 작다 can be 작을지, 작았는지, or 작은지.

마땅하다 = "to be right," "to be appropriate"
편지지 = "stationary paper"
~지 모르겠다 = "to not know whether/if…"

자기 전에 청소도 좀 할 겸 책상 서랍에 있는 것들을 다 꺼내봐야지.

"Before sleeping I'd better do a little cleaning also, as well as taking everything out of the drawers in my desk."

Attaching ~기 전에 to an action verb stem means "before doing" something.

The grammar form ~(을/ㄹ) 겸 attaches to action verb stems to mean that two actions are completed together (at around the same time) and for the same purpose – like "killing two birds with one stone." For example, you could say 한국어 공부도 하고 한국인 친구도 만날 겸 한국에 가고 싶어요 ("I want to go to Korea to study Korean too and also meet Korean friends.").

The ~야지 ending on 꺼내봐야지 adds the meaning of "have to" and is a shortened version of ~야 되지 or ~야 하지. As such, it is casual and can also translate as "I better" or "I gotta." Note that this attaches to conjugated verbs, so 하다 would become 해야지 (not 하야지).

~기 전에 = "before doing"
~(을/ㄹ) 겸 = (two actions for the same purpose)
서랍 = "drawer"
꺼내다 = "to take out," "to pull out"
~야지 = "better," "gotta," "have to"

어머니께서 마음에 들어 하시면 좋겠다.

"I hope that my mother likes it."

어머니께서 has the same meaning as 어머니가. 께서 is the honorific version of the Subject Marker (이/가) and can be attached to other people (not yourself) when using honorifics. The honorific version of the Topic Marker (은/는) is 께서는.

친구와 함께 고른 선물

마음에 들다 literally means that something "enters" (들다) your "heart" (마음), and therefore whatever you like using 마음에 들다 can't be marked with the Object Marker (을/를). This expression is often used to say that you like something when you see it for the first time, and therefore it's used for describing that you "like" something based on your first impressions of it.

When talking about what a 3rd person ("he/she/they") wants, desires, and feels (their emotions), most regular verbs can't be used without first modifying them. For example, 가고 싶다 can only apply to "me" or "you" wanting to go (가다), but not when talking about "him/her/they." Instead, attach ~(아/어/etc.) 하다 to the end of the conjugated verb. For an example of this, 가고 싶다 can be used to talk about a 3rd person by changing to 가고 싶어하다, and 마음에 들다 can become 마음에 들어 하다 (here, as the honorific version 마음에 들어 하시다).

The grammar form ~(으)면 좋겠다 literally means "it would be good if" someone does something. It's commonly used to mean "I hope" or "I wish" that someone would do something, or that something would be a certain way – for example, 빨리 봄이 오면 좋겠어요 ("I hope spring comes quickly."). It's more commonly used with a verb conjugated in the past tense, which shows a stronger hope or wish – 빨리 봄이 왔으면 좋겠어요.

~께서 = Subject Marker (이/가) (honorific)
~께서는 = Topic Marker (은/는) (honorific)
마음에 들다 = "to like"
~(아/어/etc.) 하다 = 3rd person verbs (wants, desires, emotions)
~(으)면 좋겠다 = "I hope...," "I wish..."

엄마랑 데이트

오늘은 오랜만에 엄마와 둘이서 데이트를 했다.
아침 일찍 나와서 한남동에 있는 카페에 갔는데 거기서 연예인을 3명이나
봤다. 평생 연예인 실물을 본 적이 없는데 하루에 3명이나 보다니 너무
신기했다. 특히 요즘 드라마로 인기몰이 중인 영희! 메이크업도 안 하고 대충
아무거나 입고서 커피 사러 나온 건데도 미모는 가려지지 않더라.
후광이 비친다는 게 이런 거구나 싶었다. 내가 연예인 보고 신기해하니까
엄마가 결혼 전에 남자 배우랑 만날 뻔했다고 하셨는데, 과연 그게
진짜일까? 카페에서 나와서 점심은 엄마가 노래를 부르던 떡볶이!
역시 떡볶이는 밀떡이 최고지. 그러고 나서 영화도 보고 액세서리 가게도
여러 군데 구경하고 엄마랑 커플 목걸이도 샀다.
저녁은 내가 아르바이트해서 모은 돈으로 호텔 식당에 갔다.
아무래도 내 입맛엔 떡볶이가 더 맛있었지만 엄마가 좋아하셨으니 뭐….
엄마랑 얘기도 많이 하고 재미있던 하루였다.

엄마랑 데이트

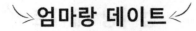

엄마랑 데이트
"A date with mom."

오늘은 오랜만에 엄마와 둘이서 데이트를 했다.
"Today I went on a date with my mom for the first time in a while, just the two of us."

오랜만에 (from 오래간만 and the particle 에) is used to say that a long time has passed since something happened. In this way, it can translate as "after a long time" or "for the first time in a long time." 오랜만 is also used in the common expression 오랜만이에요 ("Long time no see."), which literally means "it has been a long time since (we last met)."

둘이서 is a combination of 둘이 (meaning "two people") and the particle (에)서. It means "as two people," and is used to mean "together (as two people)" or "just the two of us (or them)." If there are three or four people, use 셋이서 ("the three of") or 넷이서 ("the four of").

오랜만에 = "after a long time," "(for the first time) in a long time"
둘이서 = "the two of," "together (as two)"
셋이서 = "the three of," "together (as three)"
넷이서 = "the four of," "together (as four)"
데이트(를) 하다 = "to (go on a) date"

아침 일찍 나와서 한남동에 있는 카페에 갔는데 거기서 연예인을 3 명이나 봤다.
"We left early in the morning and went to a cafe in Hannam-dong, and there saw at least three celebrities."

일찍 나오다 literally means "to come out early," and is referring to leaving the house early (in the morning).

한남동 is the name of a neighborhood – the 동 is used to refer to the name of a specific (usually small) neighborhood within a larger district. Districts are named with the ending 구 ("district"), and are administrative sections of cities.

동 = "neighborhood (in a district)"
구 = "district (of a city)"
연예인 = "celebrity," "performer"

평생 연예인 실물을 본 적이 없는데 하루에 3 명이나 보다니 너무 신기했다.
"I haven't seen a real celebrity in my entire life, so it was so cool seeing like three in one day."

~다니 can be attached to a verb stem to show an emotional reaction to hearing about something; it's often followed by an emotion or thought. In the example, the speaker uses 보다니 to show an emotional reaction to seeing three celebrities, and their reaction to that was 너무 신기했다 ("it was so cool").

While (이)나 can be used to mean "or something" or "or somewhere," it can also be attached by itself (without a second noun) to just mean "about" or "as many as" or even just "like" when used as an approximation.

평생 = "(in) one's whole life"
실물 = "real (thing, person)," "genuine (thing, person)"
~다니 = (showing an emotional reaction)
신기하다 = "to be awesome," "to be amazing"

특히 요즘 드라마로 인기몰이 중인 영희!
"Especially Yung-hee, who's currently gaining popularity from her recent drama show."

중인 is a combination of 중 ("middle" or "in the middle of") and 이다 ("to be"). 중 is often added after nouns to mean currently "in the middle of (doing noun)." Alternatively, it can also be used after action verb stems by attaching 는 to mean "in the middle of (doing verb)." For example, 하다 can become 하는 중이다 ("to be in the middle of doing"). Together, 인기몰이 중이다 means "to be in the middle of gaining popularity." Here, 중이다 is used as an adjective (중인) to describe 영희.

특히 = "particularly," "especially"
드라마 = "drama (show)"
인기몰이 = "gaining popularity," "becoming a hit"
중이다 = "to be in the middle of doing"

메이크업도 안 하고 대충 아무거나 입고서 커피 사러 나온 건데도 미모는 가려지지 않더라.
"Even though she didn't have any makeup on and wasn't wearing anything special and came out to buy coffee, (I recall) she couldn't hide her beauty."

대충 is an adverb used to show that something is "approximately" or "roughly" a certain amount, or to show that someone does something "sloppily" or "without care." 대충 아무거나 입다 is being used here to mean "to wear whatever without caring (what it is)."

The ~고서 ending can be attached after an action verb stem to show that something happens after doing something else, similar to saying "and (then)." ~고서 has the same usage as ~고 나서.

The 데도 at the end of 나온 건데도 is 나온 것인데도, a combination of 것 with 이다 in the 데 form – here as 인데 – with the particle 도 ("also," "too," "even"); it means "even though."

가려지다 is the passive verb form of 가리다 ("to hide," "to cover"). In the example, 미모는 가려지지 않더라 literally means "her beauty was not hidden." Since the passive voice in Korean is also often used to mean "can" and "can't" – such as in the common passive verbs 보이다 and 들리다 – a more natural translation would be "(she) couldn't hide her beauty."

The ~더라 ending is a colloquial, informal version of ~더라고. They have the same meaning, and are both used to express surprise toward something in the past that you personally experienced, realized, saw happening, or found out – in this sentence, the speaker is expressing her surprise about the experience of personally seeing the celebrity's face.

메이크업(을) 하다 = "to put on makeup," "to wear makeup"
대충 = "approximately," "roughly," "of sorts," "sloppily," "without care"
아무거나 = "whatever," "anything"
~고 나서 = "and then," "after (doing)"
~고서 = ~고 나서
미모 = "(one's) beauty," "pretty face," "pretty looks," "pretty features"
가려지다 = "to be hidden," "to be covered"
가리다 = "to hide," "to cover"

후광이 비친다는 게 이런 거구나 싶었다.
"I wondered if this is what they call having a halo."

후광 is a halo of light, often depicted in Buddhist artwork and teachings. To say that someone has a halo around their head or that an object has a halo around it use 후광(이) 비치다 – literally, "a halo shines."

The ~구나 ending is used when the speaker realizes something that they didn't know, and is only for casual speech; use ~구나 after descriptive verb stems and ~는구나 after action verb stems. For other non-casual situations, ~군 or ~군요 can be used in the same way. 이런 거구나 is a shortened version of 이런 것이구나.

The ~나 싶다 ending can be attached to a verb stem to show that you're wondering something to yourself – not asking someone else. This form is a combination of the ~나(요) ending which shows that you're extra curious to know the answer to a question, along with the verb 싶다 ("to think about," "to worry about").

후광 = "(Buddhist) halo"
비치다 = "to shine"
후광(이) 비치다 = "to have a halo"
~구나 = (realizing something)
~나 싶다 = "to wonder (to oneself) if"

내가 연예인 보고 신기해하니까 엄마가 결혼 전에 남자 배우랑 만날 뻔했다고 하셨는데, 과연 그게 진짜일까?
"Because I was amazed at seeing a celebrity, my mom said that she almost met a male actor before getting married, but would that really be true?"

Attaching 하다 to a conjugated descriptive verb – here, 신기해하다 – can also add the meaning of "to feel" to the verb. Here, 신기해하다 (from 신기하다) means "to feel amazed."

엄마랑 데이트

전 ("before") and 후 ("after") can not only be attached after verbs, but also directly after nouns. 결혼 전 ("before marriage") and 결혼하기 전에 ("before getting married") would both have similar meanings.

만나다 ("to meet") can also be used to mean "to meet (for dating)" or "to go out with."

과연 ("really," "indeed") is an adverb that's most often used together with the ~까(요) ending. It's used to express the meaning of "really" when you are suspicious of whether something is true or not.

~(아/어/etc.) 하다 = "to feel (descriptive verb)"
배우 = "actor"
과연 = "really," "indeed"

카페에서 나와서 점심은 엄마가 노래를 부르던 떡볶이!
"We came out of the cafe and then for lunch we had spicy rice cakes, which my mom was singing about!"

When using ~던 after an action verb stem, it means that action used to happen in the past – 엄마가 노래를 부르던 떡볶이 means "spicy rice cakes that my mom used to sing about" or "spicy rice cakes that my mom was singing about." It's used to emphasize that the action happened repeatedly, or over a period of time; in this case, mom was likely singing about spicy rice cakes throughout the day, and for lunch they finally went to eat some. Using ~던 after an action verb stem in the past tense would also have a similar meaning, but emphasizes that although the action happened in the past it no longer happens now; 엄마가 노래를 불렀던 떡볶이 would instead have the meaning of "the spicy rice cakes that my mom used to sing about in the past, but no longer does."

~던 = (repeatedly used to happen)

역시 떡볶이는 밀떡이 최고지.
"Of course when it comes to spicy rice cakes, wheat flour cakes are the best."

역시 is an adverb used to show that something is as you've expected, or just as you already knew it to be – "Just as I expected!" A more common way to translate it can be "of course" or even "after all."

Most 떡볶이 ("spicy rice cakes") sold on the streets and in restaurants is actually made using 밀떡 ("wheat flour cakes"). 떡볶이 made with wheat flour is softer and chewier, while 떡볶이 made with 쌀떡 ("rice flour cakes") is firmer and can be chewed longer. Both kinds are used and enjoyed in Korea.

역시 = "as (one) expected," "as (one) knew," "of course"
밀떡 = "wheat flour cakes"
쌀떡 = "rice flour cakes"

엄마랑 데이트

그러고 나서 영화도 보고 액세서리 가게도 여러 군데 구경하고 엄마랑 커플 목걸이도 샀다.

"After that we also watched a movie and looked around several accessory stores too, and I also bought matching necklaces with my mom."

액세서리 가게도 여러 군데(를) 구경하다 literally means "to look around accessory stores also, several places." 여러 군데 is being used here as a counter for how many accessory stores they went to. Had they only visited three places, it could have said 세 군데 ("three places") instead.

커플 ("couple") can be used as an adjective to describe two matching objects, often bought by couples who are in a relationship. 커플 목걸이 could either translate as "couple necklaces" or just "matching necklaces." Another common "couple" item is 커플 반지 ("couple rings"), although shirts, shoes, and occasionally entire wardrobes are not uncommon.

그러고 나서 = "after (doing) that," "next"
액세서리 = "accessory"
군데 = "place," "spot," place counter
구경(을) 하다 = "to look around," "to see"
커플 = "couple," "two people (in a relationship)"
목걸이 = "necklace"

저녁은 내가 아르바이트해서 모은 돈으로 호텔 식당에 갔다.

"For dinner we went to a hotel restaurant with money I saved up working a part-time job."

모으다 = "to gather," "to save up (money)"

아무래도 내 입맛엔 떡볶이가 더 맛있었지만 엄마가 좋아하셨으니 뭐....

"Either way the spicy rice cakes tasted better to me (than the hotel food), but my mom liked it so whatever."

아무래도 comes from 아무리 해도, meaning "no matter how much (you or I) do it," is used at the very beginning of a sentence and means "anyway" or "either way."

좋아하셨으니 is a slightly more formal version of 좋아하셨으니까. Both the ~(으)니 ending and the ~(으)니까 ending can be used to mean "because."

내 입맛에 – written here as 내 입맛엔 (에는) – literally means "in my taste," and 입맛 is used when talking about your personal preferences for eating or drinking.

When used at the very end of a sentence, 뭐 can add the feeling of "(so) whatever" or "anyway." It's used to express that something is a certain way and can't be changed – so why fight it?

아무래도 = "anyway," "either way"
입맛 = "(one's) taste," "(one's) palate"
뭐 = "(so) whatever," "anyway"

엄마랑 얘기도 많이 하고 재미있던 하루였다.
"I also talked with my mom a lot, and it was a fun day."

하루 is often used in place of 날 ("day") when specifically talking about one day. In this example, the speaker is talking all about their one day going on a date with their mom.

하루 = "(one) day"

겨울 바다

역시 겨울 바다는 진리다.
와, 진짜 누가 21 학점이 껌이라고 했는지 정말.
이번 학기에 21 학점을 수강하느라고 시외로 나가 보기는커녕 학교 기숙사의자랑 한 몸이 되어버리는 줄 알았다. 그 와중에 수업 똑같이 들으면서 연애까지 한 지민은 분명 사람이 아닐 거다. 3일 밤새워서 시험 끝내고 같은 기숙사방 친구들이랑 동해로 무작정 놀러 갔다.
가는 날이 장날이라고 했던가 딱 축제날이어서 먹을 것도 많고 사람들도 많아서 너무 재미있었다. 특히 도루묵. 태어나서 처음 보고 처음 먹어 본 건데 앞으로는 내 인생 생선이다. 분명히 엄청 추웠는데 기억에 남는 건 시원한 바다 냄새랑 파도 소리뿐이다. 이래서 다들 겨울 바다, 겨울 바다 하는 거겠지. 원래는 안 가고 자려고 했는데 억지로 끌고 가준 철수야 고맙다. 앞으로 네 말이라면 팥으로 메주를 쑨다고 해도 믿고 따를게!

겨울 바다

겨울 바다

"The winter sea."

겨울 바다 means "winter sea" or "sea in wintertime."

겨울 바다 = "winter sea"

역시 겨울 바다는 진리다.

"Of course the winter sea is the best."

진리 means "truth," but it can also be used as a slang word to mean that something is "the best" (similar to 최고).

진리 = "truth," "the best"

와, 진짜 누가 21 학점이 껌이라고 했는지 정말.

"Wow, seriously who said that 21 credits would be a piece of cake? Come on."

Typically Korean university students will take between 18 and 21 credits (학점) – the more they take, the harder it is and the more work they have to complete.

껌 ("gum") can also be used to say that something is extremely easy, like "a piece of cake;" this is used to say that something is as easy as chewing gum. When used this way, it's followed by 이다 ("to be") as 껌이다 ("to be a piece of cake").

Both 진짜 and 정말 can translate as "really" or "for real," but when used on their own (not with a verb) to complain about something they can also carry the emotion of the expressions "Come on" or "Are you kidding me?"

학점 = "(school) credit"
껌 = "gum"
껌이다 = "to be a piece of cake"

이번 학기에 21 학점을 수강하느라고 시외로 나가 보기는커녕 학교 기숙사 의자랑 한 몸이 되어버리는 줄 알았다.

"Because I'm taking 21 credits this semester, forget going out to the countryside. I thought I was becoming one with my chair at the school dormitory."

You can attach ~느라고 to a present tense action verb stem to mean "because" or "due to" something you did; this is only used to talk about something negative (not when something good happens). Using ~느라고 for 수강하느라고 shows that the writer regrets having taken the classes (likely because of how difficult they were).

커녕 is used to compare two facts by emphasizing the fact that comes after the first one (marked with 커녕). To use it, take a noun and attach 는 (after a vowel) or 은 (after a consonant) followed by 커녕; this can translate as "let alone (noun)..." or "rather than (noun)...." In casual usage, this can also translate to "forget (noun)...."

한 몸 literally means "one body," and together with 되다 ("to become") it means "to become one (with)." Here, the writer is expressing they were sitting in their chair for so long that they felt they were becoming fused to it.

버리다 ("to throw away") can be attached after a conjugated action verb to add extra emotion to a sentence, and to show that the action has completed. It's often used when complaining about something due to sadness or disappointment. Here, 되어버리다 (from 되다) shows they felt sad at becoming one with their chair..

The ~줄(을) 알다 form is attached after conjugating a verb to an adjective and is used to say you had an expectation about something - this can be either "to think" or "to know" depending on the context.

학기 = "(school) semester"
수강(을) 하다 = "to take a course," "to take a class"
~느라고 = "because," "due to" (negative outcome)
시외 = "outside the city," "countryside"
~(은/는)커녕 = "let alone...," "rather than...," "forget..."
기숙사 = "dormitory"
한 몸 = "one (body)"
~줄(을) 알다 = "to think (that)," "to know (that)," "to expect (that)"

그 와중에 수업 똑같이 들으면서 연애까지 한 지민은 분명 사람이 아닐 거다.

"Meanwhile there's Jimin who while taking the same classes as me even had a boyfriend. She's clearly not human."

똑같이 is an adverb that can be used to show that someone does an action verb in the same exact way. The sentence 수업 똑같이 들으면서 shows that Jimin took classes in the same way (the same classes) as the writer.

연애(를) 하다 means to have a romantic relationship with someone or to date, but a more natural translation could also be just "to have a boyfriend" or "to have a girlfriend."

그 와중에 = "meanwhile," "in the meantime"
똑같이 = "identically," "(just) like," "the same"
연애(를) 하다 = "to have a romantic relationship," "to go out with (someone)"
분명 = "certainly," "clearly," "obviously"

3 일 밤새워서 시험 끝내고 같은 기숙사방 친구들이랑 동해로 무작정 놀러 갔다.

"I stayed up for 3 days and finished my tests, then without any plans went to the East Sea to hang out with my friends from the same dormitory room."

겨울 바다

동해 literally means "East Sea," and it refers to the ocean area east from Korea.

밤(을) 새우다 = "to stay up all night"
기숙사방 = "dormitory room"
동해 = "East Sea"
무작정 = "without any plan," "thoughtlessly," "randomly"
놀다 = "to play," "to hang out"

가는 날이 장날이라고 했던가 딱 축제날이어서 먹을 것도 많고 사람들도 많아서 너무 재미있었다.

"I don't know if it was bad timing, but it (that day exactly) was a holiday so there was also lots of food to eat, and lots of people too so it was so much fun."

가는 날이 장날이다 is an expression used to mean that something is bad or good timing. Literally 장날 means "market day," so accidentally going (가다) somewhere only to realize that it's market day (an extremely busy day) would be an example of bad timing – literally, "the day (I) go is market day."

You can attach ~던가 to the end of a verb stem when asking yourself a question about something in the past to which you don't know or can't remember the answer; in this way it's like adding "was it?" to the end of a sentence.

먹을 것 ("thing to eat") is more commonly used than the literal 먹을 음식 ("food to eat"), and has the same meaning.

~던가 = "whether it was (I don't know)..."
딱 = "just (exactly)," "perfectly"
가는 날이 장날이다 = "to be bad (or good) timing," "as luck would have it"
축제날 = "holiday," "festival day"

특히 도루묵.

"Especially sailfin sandfish."

도루묵 is a small scaleless fish that's often prepared grilled.

도루묵 = "sailfin sandfish"

태어나서 처음 보고 처음 먹어 본 건데 앞으로는 내 인생 생선이다.

"It was my first time seeing it in my life and my first time trying it, but from now on it's my favorite fish."

인생 생선 literally means "(human) life fish," but this is an exaggerated way to say that the fish (도루묵) is now a part of the writer's life – because they enjoyed it so much.

겨울 바다

태어나서 처음 = "(for) the first time ever in my life"
앞으로 = "from now (on)," "in the future"
인생 = "(human) life"

분명히 엄청 추웠는데 기억에 남는 건 시원한 바다 냄새랑 파도 소리뿐이다.

"I'm certain it was freezing, but all that I remember is the smell of the cool ocean and the sound of the waves."

기억에 남다 means "to remain in (one's) memory" and is used to say that a memory still remains (because it was memorable).

파도 소리뿐이다 means "only the sound of the waves." You can attach ~뿐 ("only, and nothing more") with 이다 ("to be") after a noun to mean "all it is, is..." or "it's just...." Similarly, you might also find ~일뿐이다 (일 from 이다) after a noun; this has the same meaning but is used when complaining about the noun or talking about the noun in a negative way.

엄청 = "very," "terribly," "seriously," "awfully"
기억에 남다 = "to remain in (one's) memory," "to be memorable"
분명히 = "clearly," "certainly," "plainly," "definitely"
파도 = "(water) wave"
~뿐이다 = "all it is, is...," "it's just..."
~일뿐이다 = "all it is, is...," "it's just..." (negative meaning)

이래서 다들 겨울 바다, 겨울 바다 하는 거겠지.

"So that must be why everyone says the winter sea."

Just how 그래서 comes from 그렇다 ("to be like that," "to be so"), 이래서 comes from 이렇다 ("to be like this," "to be so"). It's used to show that the reason that follows is a result of "this" – "therefore (because of this)."

겨울 바다 is repeated twice to show emphasis, as if saying (or talking about) – here, 하다 means 말(을) 하다 – something two times. You can also think of this usage here as meaning "everyone talks about the winter sea."

이래서 = "therefore," "so"
다들 = "everybody," "everyone"

원래는 안 가고 자려고 했는데 억지로 끌고 가준 철수야 고맙다.

"Originally I was going to sleep and not go, but I'm thankful to Chul-soo who dragged me along and forced me to go."

You can use 억지로 with a verb to mean that someone forces someone to do something. 억지로 끌고 가다 means "to drag (someone) along by force" or "to force someone to go."

겨울 바다

When calling out to a friend to get their attention, attach 야 after their first name if it ends in a consonant, or attach 아 after their first name if it ends in a vowel. Here, the writer is calling out to Chul-soo as if saying, "Chul-soo, thank you."

원래 = "originally," "always (from the beginning)"
억지로 = "against one's will," "by force," "forcefully"
끌다 = "to pull," "to drag (along)"
끌고 가다 = "to drag (along) somewhere"

앞으로 네 말이라면 팥으로 메주를 쑨다고 해도 믿고 따를게!
"From now on if you say so, no matter what you say I'll believe you and follow you."

네 말이라면 literally means "if it's your word," and it can be used to mean "if it's something that you said" or just "if you say so." Note that 네 (from 너의) is only appropriate in casual speech with close friends.

메주 is a block of dried and fermented soybeans, which is then used in recipes to make 고추장, 된장, 간장, and more. 메주(를) 쑤다 is to prepare the block of fermented soybeans by boiling it in water. Normally 메주 is prepared with soybeans, but if you were to make 메주 with red (adzuki) beans it would sound strange and wrong. The expression 팥으로 메주(를) 쑨다 해도 literally means "even if you say that you're making a block of dried fermented soybeans using red (adzuki) beans" and is used to show that you have complete confidence in someone – even if what they're saying makes no sense.

팥 = "red (adzuki) beans"
메주 = "block of dried fermented soybeans"
쑤다 = "to cook grains (by boiling)"
팥으로 메주(를) 쑨다 해도 믿겠다 = "No matter what you say, (I) will believe you."
따르다 = "to follow"

서울 한복판에 놀이공원 연상케 하는 대형 서점 개점

다국적 대기업 C 기업에서 3 년간의 준비 끝에 놀이공원을 연상케 하는 대형 서점을 개점하여 많은 학부모들과 학생들의 이목을 끌고 있다. 이 대형 서점은 5 층짜리 건물로 각 층마다 다른 테마를 가지고 있으며 학생들 사이에서 인기 있는 책들의 배경을 그대로 본떠 매우 흥미롭다는 평가이다. 이 새로운 서점의 매니저이자 국내 인기 작가로 활동 중인 김 박사는 "글로만 읽어서는 부족할 수 있는 어린이들과 십 대 청소년들의 상상력을 일깨워주고 창의력을 증진시키는 데에 도움이 될 것"이라며 "학생들이 교과서와 컴퓨터에서 벗어나 뇌에 건강한 자극을 줄 수 있길 바란다"라고 말했다. 이 서점에는 유치원 어린이부터 초등학교 저학년 학생들이 책 속 내용을 실제로 체험해 볼 수 있는 놀이기구들도 준비되어 있어 많은 가족들이 찾을 것으로 기대된다.

[고빌리 신문 제미 기자 J-gija@gobillykorean.com]

서울 한복판에 놀이공원 연상케 하는 대형 서점 개점

"Opening of Large Bookstore Reminiscent of an Amusement Park in the Heart of Seoul"

한복판 (or 복판) can be used to mean the "very center" of somewhere, or "heart."

The standard ~하게 ending can shorten to just ~케 in some verbs (but not all); 연상케 하는 is a shortening of 연상하게 하는 ("reminiscent"), from 연상하다 ("to be reminiscent of something").

In order to save space and for stylistic reasons, article titles in Korean (and English) are often not complete sentences – this title simply ends in 서점 개점 ("opening of a bookstore").

(한)복판 = "the (very) center," "the heart (of somewhere)"
놀이공원 = "amusement park"
연상(을) 하다 = "to be reminiscent of something"
연상(을) 하게 하다 = "to remind"
~케 = ~하게
대형 = "large size"
서점 = "bookstore"
개점 = "opening (of a store)"

서울 한복판에 놀이공원 연상케 하는 대형 서점 개점

다국적 대기업 C 기업에서 3 년간의 준비 끝에 놀이공원을 연상케 하는 대형 서점을 개점하여 많은 학부모들과 학생들의 이목을 끌고 있다.

"At the end of 3 years of preparation, the multinational conglomerate company 'C' opens a large bookstore reminiscent of an amusement park, attracting the attention of many parents and students."

다국적 comes from 다, a Sino-Korean word meaning "multi" or "many," and 국적 ("national"). Together, it means "multinational."

대기업 comes from 대, a Sino-Korean word meaning "large," and 기업 ("corporation").

간 can be attached after a period of time (a time counter), and has the same meaning as 동안 ("for," "while"). Both 3 년간 and 3 년 동안 mean "for/during 3 years."

하여 is a slightly formal-sounding older conjugation of 해 from the verb 하다; it has the same meaning as 해(서). 하여 most often only appears in writing.

학부모 is a combination of the Sino-Korean word 학 meaning "school" or "learning," and 부모 ("parents"). Together, it means the "parents (or guardians) of students."

끌다 ("to pull") can be used with 이목 ("attention") to literally mean "to pull attention" or "to attract attention."

다국적 = "multinational"
기업 = "company," "business"
대기업 = "large corporation," "conglomerate"
~간 = "for," "during" (after counter)
하여 = 해(서)
끝에 = "at the end," "at the close"
학부모 = "parents (or guardians) of students"
이목 = "attention"
이목(을) 끌다 = "to attract attention"

이 대형 서점은 5 층짜리 건물로 각 층마다 다른 테마를 가지고 있으며 학생들 사이에서 인기 있는 책들의 배경을 그대로 본떠 매우 흥미롭다는 평가이다.

"This large bookstore has received high praise for having a different theme for each floor of its 5-story building which is modeled exactly after the backgrounds of books that are popular among students, and for being extremely interesting to look at."

층 is a counter used for "floors" or "stories" of a building, and follows after a Sino-Korean number. ~짜리 can be attached after a counter to mean "worth (of)" or "amount (of)" – it can then be followed by a noun. (#)층짜리 건물 means "a building that has (#) floors."

각 is a Sino-Korean word that attaches to the front of words and means "each," so 각 층 means "each floor." For additional emphasis, it's commonly used together with the ending 마다 which also means "each."

Since ~(으)며 has a similar meaning as the ~고 verb ending, 가지고 있으며 has the same meaning as 가지고 있고.

사이 means "between," and 사이에서 attached to a noun means "among (noun)."

그대로 is an adverb that means "as something is" or "(just/exactly) as it is." Combined with 본(을) 뜨다 – here conjugated as 본떠 – which means "to copy (something)" or "to be modeled after (something)" means "to be exactly modeled after (something)."

평가 means "review" or "rating," and is used at the end of the sentence to show that the bookstore is reviewed by the public in this way (following the Plain Form). Although a literal translation would be "is reviewed as," for a more natural translation you can also think of this form (Plain Form + 평가이다) as meaning "to receive (high) praise for."

층 = (building) floor counter
~짜리 = "worth (of)," "amount (of)"
각 = "each" (prefix)
마다 = "each" (suffix)
테마 = "theme"
사이 = "between"
사이에서 = "among (noun)"
배경 = "background"
그대로 = "(just/exactly) as it is"
본(을) 뜨다 = "to copy (something)," "to be modeled after (something)"
평가 = "review," "rating"

이 새로운 서점의 매니저이자 국내 인기 작가로 활동 중인 김 박사는 "글로만 읽어서는 부족할 수 있는 어린이들과 십 대 청소년들의 상상력을 일깨워주고 창의력을 증진시키는 데에 도움이 될 것"이라며 "학생들이 교과서와 컴퓨터에서 벗어나 뇌에 건강한 자극을 줄 수 있길 바란다"라고 말했다.

"Doctor Kim, the manager of this new bookstore and currently working as a popular author in Korea said, 'It will help to enhance creativity and awaken the imaginations of teenagers and children who need more than just books,' and 'I hope that students will break away from textbooks and computers, and give their minds healthy stimulation.'"

이자 comes from 이다 ("to be"), and is used to connect two current states of something that happen at the same time. It's commonly used to show that a person is holding two responsibilities at once.

국내 means "domestic," but since this article takes place in a Seoul bookstore, "Korean author" is a much more natural translation. 국내 is often used in this way to mean "Korean" when referring to something within Korea.

활동 중 is a combination of 활동 ("activity") and 중 ("middle") and means "in the middle of doing (working on) something."

The sentence 글로만 is 글 ("writing," "letters") and (으)로 ("using") with 만 ("only"). 읽어서는 is 읽다 ("to read") with the ~서 form, and the Topic Marker (은/는). Combined with 부족할 수 있다 from 부족하다 ("to be insufficient") it means "only (by) reading books might not be enough."

대 means "generation," and 십 대 literally means "10 generation." This is used to refer to "teenagers" (people in their 10s).

증진시키는 데 uses 증진(을) 시키다 ("to enhance," "to increase") and the noun 데 ("place"), which is conjugated the same way as the ~데 verb ending (but with a space). It can be used after a verb in this way to mean "(in order) to," so 증진시키는 데 means "(in order) to increase/enhance." This 데 form has a similar meaning as 위해(서), but is more commonly used.

~(이)라며 comes from (이)라고 하며, and uses (으)며 which is a written form that's similar in meaning to the ~고 verb ending. Here it has the same meaning as (이)라고 (말)하고.

~기(를) 바라다 can be used after a verb stem to show that you "hope" or "wish" for something. Often 기를 will be contracted to just 길.

~(이)자 = "and" (for connecting states)
국내 = "domestic"
활동 = "activity"
박사 = "doctor (Ph.D.)"
대 = generation counter
십 대 = "teenagers"
청소년 = "adolescent," "youth"
상상력 = "imagination"
일깨우다 = "to awaken," "to enlighten"
창의력 = "creativity"
증진(을) 시키다 = "to enhance," "to increase"
데 = "place"
~데 = "(in order) to"
도움(이) 되다 = "to be helpful"
벗어나다 = "to get out (of)," "to break away (from)"
자극 = "stimulus," "stimulation"
바라다 = "to hope," "to wish"
~길 = ~기를
~기(를) 바라다 = "to hope (that)," "to wish (that)"

서울 한복판에 놀이공원 연상케 하는 대형 서점 개점

이 서점에는 유치원 어린이부터 초등학교 저학년 학생들이 책 속 내용을 실제로 체험해 볼 수 있는 놀이기구들도 준비되어 있어 많은 가족들이 찾을 것으로 기대된다.

"In this bookstore, rides are also prepared for preschool children to new elementary school students to be able to actually experience firsthand the contents inside of books, and many families are expected to visit."

저학년 is a combination of the Sino-Korean word 저 ("low") and 학년 ("school year"). 학년 can be used after a Sino-Korean number to express a specific school year. 초등학교 저학년 means "the first 1-3 years of elementary school."

속 means "inside," but is typically used to refer to the "deep inside" of things that you don't physically go inside (e.g. deep in your mind, deep in a forest, deep into a mountainous area). 안 ("inside") is used for anything with a physical inside. 책 속 means "inside of books," and is referring to the contents of the books.

준비되어 있다 uses the passive verb 준비(가) 되다 ("to be prepared") and the grammar form ~(아/어/etc.) 있다, which shows that something is currently in a certain state – here, the state of having been "prepared."

찾다 ("to look for," "to find") can also be used to mean "to visit (somewhere)." In this way it's like saying "to find (and visit) this bookstore."

기대(가) 되다 means "to be expected," and (으)로 is used to show what is being expected. In this sentence, 많은 가족들이 찾을 것 means "(that/for) many families to visit."

유치원 = "preschool"
초등학교 저학년 = "the first 1-3 years of elementary school"
속 = "(deep) inside"
내용 = "contents"
체험(을) 하다 = "to experience (firsthand)"
놀이기구 = "(amusement) ride"
준비(가) 되다 = "to be prepared"
찾다 = "to look for," "to find," "to visit (somewhere)"
기대(가) 되다 = "to be expected"

[고빌리 신문 제미 기자 J-gija@gobillykorean.com]

"GoBilly News, Reporter Jemi"

Remember that Korean uses titles together with names. In this case, 제미 is a reporter, so they wrote 제미 기자 as their name. News articles will always end with the name of the newspaper reporter listed in a similar fashion.

기자 = "(news) reporter"

태풍 곰 발바닥의 영향으로 전국 많은 비

오늘은 태풍 곰 발바닥의 영향으로 전국적으로 비가 내리겠습니다. 강수량은 중부 지방 50~80mm, 남부 지방도 최고 80mm 정도로 많은 비가 올 것으로 예상됩니다. 특히 남부 일부 지역은 며칠째 지속된 비로 지반 약화로 인한 피해가 발생하지 않도록 각별한 주의가 필요합니다. 오늘 낮 기온은 서울이 11 도 대전이 13 도 부산이 15 도 등으로 어제와 비슷하거나 조금 높겠습니다. 바다의 물결은 모든 해상 먼바다에서 3 에서 6 미터로 높게 일겠습니다. 기상청에서는 해안지역에서 외출을 자제하시길 권고했습니다. 태풍 곰 발바닥은 빠른 속도로 북상하고 있으며 우리나라에는 앞으로 최소 3 일간 더 영향을 줄 것으로 전망하고 있습니다.

[고빌리 신문 제미 기자 J-gija@gobillykorean.com]

태풍 곰 발바닥의 영향으로 전국 많은 비

"Lots of rain over the whole country due to the effect of Typhoon Bear Paw."

발바닥 literally means "foot floor" and is used to refer to the flat bottom area of a foot. This can be a person's palm, or an animal's paw. 태풍 곰 발바닥 ("Typhoon Bear Paw") is a fictitious typhoon name used in this article.

You can use 영향 with (으)로 to mean "due to the effect," "due to the influence," or "as a result" of something. Mark the noun before it with the Possessive Marker (의).

Note how the title of the news article is not a complete sentence. Literally it would translate to "Due to Typhoon Bear Paw whole country lots of rain."

태풍 = "typhoon"
발바닥 = "palm," "paw"
영향 = "influence," "effect"
~의 영향으로 = "due to...," "as a result of"
전국 = "whole country," "whole nation"

태풍 곰 발바닥의 영향으로 전국 많은 비

오늘은 태풍 곰 발바닥의 영향으로 전국적으로 비가 내리겠습니다.
"Today due to Typhoon Bear Paw it will rain nationwide."

Just like 비(가) 오다, 비(가) 내리다 also means "to rain." 비(가) 내리다 is very slightly more formal, but both expressions are commonly used.

전국적으로 = "nationally," "nationwide," "all over the (whole) country"
비(가) 내리다 = "to rain"

강수량은 중부 지방 50~80mm, 남부 지방도 최고 80mm 정도로 많은 비가 올 것으로 예상됩니다.
"The amount of rainfall is expected to be approximately 50-80mm in the central region as well as at most 80mm in the southern region."

중부 지방 means the central region of a country. For Korea, the central region would include the areas near 서울. The northern region would be everywhere above there, and the southern region would be everywhere below there.

The "~" symbol in "50~80mm" would be read aloud as "50 에서 80," using 에서 ("from").

"최고 80mm" means "80mm at most." The opposite of 최고 would be 최저 ("minimum," "the lowest").

예상 means an expectation, a prediction, or a forecast. When used as a verb, it can become either 예상(을) 하다 or 예상(이) 되다. Here, it's used together with the particle (으)로 to mean "to be expected/forecasted/predicted as...."

강수량 = "rainfall (amount)"
북부 지방 = "northern region"
중부 지방 = "central region"
남부 지방 = "southern region"
최고 = "maximum," "at most," "(the) best"
최저 = "minimum," "the lowest"
예상 = "expectation," "prediction," "forecast"
예상(이) 되다 = "to be expected," "to be forecasted," "to be predicted"
예상(을) 하다 = "to expect," "to forecast," "to predict"

특히 남부 일부 지역은 며칠째 지속된 비로 지반 약화로 인한 피해가 발생하지 않도록 각별한 주의가 필요합니다.
"Particularly in some southern regions, special caution is necessary in order for damage to not occur due to the ground weakening by the continued rain for the past few days."

(으)로 can also be used to show the cause or the reason of something, similar to "by" – in the sentence, 지속된 비로 means "by the continued rain" or "because of the continued rain."

(으)로 인하다 also has a similar usage to show the direct result of something. It's used after a noun followed by the particle (으)로, and can be conjugated in several ways. When used as an adjective conjugate it to 인한, and when used as an adverb conjugate it to 인해(서). In the sentence, 지반 약화로 인한 피해 means "damage (that is) as a result of the ground weakening."

~도록 means "so that" or "in order to," and attaches directly to a verb stem. 피해가 발생하지 않도록 can translate as either "so that damage does not occur" or "in order for damage to not occur."

Note that 필요하다 means "to be necessary" and is a descriptive verb – it does not use an Object Marker (을/를).

일부 지역 = "some areas," "some regions"
며칠째 = "for a few days," "for the past few days"
지속(이) 되다 = "to continue," "to persist"
지반 = "ground (surface)"
약화 = "weakening"
(으)로 인하다 = "to be due to," "to be as a result of"
피해 = "damage," "harm"
발생(을) 하다 = "to occur," "to happen"
~도록 = "so that," "in order to"
각별하다 = "to be particular," "to be special"
주의 = "care," "caution"
필요하다 = "to be necessary"

오늘 낮 기온은 서울이 11 도 대전이 13 도 부산이 15 도 등으로 어제와 비슷하거나 조금 높겠습니다.

"Today's daytime temperature for Seoul is 11 degrees, Daejeon is 13 degrees, Busan is 15 degrees (etc.), and will be similar or a little higher than yesterday."

기온 means "temperature" when referring to the weather. 온도 means "temperature" when referring to an object. 체온 means "temperature" when referring to someone (to determine whether they're healthy or sick).

낮 기온 = "daytime temperature"
기온 = "(weather) temperature"
온도 = "(object) temperature"
체온 = "(body) temperature"
도 = degree counter
등으로 = "and such," "et cetera," "and so on"

바다의 물결은 모든 해상 먼바다에서 3 에서 6 미터로 높게 일겠습니다.

"The ocean tides will rise up high from 3 to 6 meters in all seas offshore."

모든 해상 means "all seas" and 먼바다 means "offshore" or "out at sea" (literally, 먼 "far" and 바다 "ocean").

태풍 곰 발바닥의 영향으로 전국 많은 비

물결 = "tide," "flow"
해상 = "sea," "on the sea"
먼바다 = "out at sea," "offshore"
일다 = "to rise (wind, water)"

기상청에서는 해안지역에서 외출을 자제하시길 권고했습니다.

"At the National Weather Service they recommend refraining from going outside at coastal areas."

자제(를) 하다 is being used here as its honorific form, 자제(를) 하시다, to refer to people honorifically – since this is a direct recommendation to people who are at coastal areas.

Note how 권고(를) 하다 is used here after 자제하시길, which is 자제(를) 하시다 changed into a noun (자제하시기) with an Object Marker (을/를) attached to the end.

기상청 = "National Weather Service," "weather center"
해안지역 = "coastal area," "coastal region"
외출 = "going out(side)"
외출(을) 하다 = "to go out(side)"
자제(를) 하다 = "to refrain from (verb)"
권고(를) 하다 = "to advise," "to urge," "to recommend"

태풍 곰 발바닥은 빠른 속도로 북상하고 있으며 우리나라에는 앞으로 최소 3 일간 더 영향을 줄 것으로 전망하고 있습니다.

"Typhoon Bear Paw is moving north at a fast speed, and we are forecasting it to have an effect in Korea for at least three more days from now."

Note how 우리나라 ("Korea") is written without a space. 우리 나라 (with a space) simply means "our country."

속도 = "speed," "velocity"
북상(을) 하다 = "to go north," "to move north"
우리나라 = "Korea" (literally, "our country")
최소 = "minimum," "at least"
전망(을) 하다 = "to forecast," "to foresee," "to predict"

[고빌리 신문 제미 기자 J-gija@gobillykorean.com]

"GoBilly News, Reporter Jemi"

빌리 건설 사랑의 연탄 2만 장 전달

추운 겨울 빌리 건설이 적극적인 사회 공헌으로 또 한 번 이목을 끌고 있다. 2005 년 창립된 빌리 건설은 창립 당시부터 전 임직원이 자발적으로 정기적인 봉사 활동에 참여하고 있는 것으로 알려져 있다. 빌리 건설은 2019 년 사회 활동을 통해 대통령 상을 수상하기도 했다. 이번 달 22 일 진행된 사랑의 연탄 봉사 활동에서는 임원들과 가족들이 참여하여 연탄 2 만 장을 서울시 곳곳의 독거노인 및 저소득 가정에 직접 전달했다. 빌리 건설은 이달 초에 사랑의 김치 나누기 행사를 개최하였으며 매달 첫째 주 금요일에는 저소득 가정에 사랑의 쌀을 20 포대씩 전달하고 있다. 이 외에도 빌리 건설의 임직원들은 다양한 사내 봉사활동 동아리를 통해 헌혈 활동, 무료 급식, 노숙인 쉼터 등 다양한 봉사활동에 지속적으로 참여하고 있다. 기업 관계자는 '더불어 사는 세상을 통해 많은 사람들의 행복이 건설되길 바란다'며 앞으로도 다양한 공헌 활동을 통해 사랑과 행복을 전달할 것이라고 말했다.

[고빌리 신문 제미 기자 J-gija@gobillykorean.com]

빌리 건설 사랑의 연탄 2 만 장 전달

"Billy Construction delivers 20,000 'Briquettes of Love.'"

Although 장 is normally used for counting flat objects such as sheets of paper, it can also be used to count other items such as t-shirts, briquettes, roof tiles, and flat food items (like 부침개).

건설 = "construction"
장 = flat object counter
연탄 = "(coal) briquette"
전달 = "delivery (of something)," "conveying (information)"
전달(을) 하다 = "to deliver (something)," "to convey (information)"

추운 겨울 빌리 건설이 적극적인 사회 공헌으로 또 한 번 이목을 끌고 있다.

"In this cold winter Billy Construction is once again attracting interest with a positive social contribution."

적극적인 is a conjugated form of 적극적이다 ("to be active and positive").

빌리 건설 사랑의 연탄 2만 장 전달

적극적이다 = "to be active and positive"
사회 = "society," "community"
공헌 = "contribution"
사회 공헌 = "social contribution"
또 한 번 = "once (more) again"

2005 년 창립된 빌리 건설은 창립 당시부터 전 임직원이 자발적으로 정기적인 봉사 활동에 참여하고 있는 것으로 알려져 있다.

"Billy Construction was founded in 2005, and it's well known that all employees have participated in regular voluntary service projects since the time it was established."

창립 is specifically used for the foundation or establishment of a company or organization.

당시 is commonly used as 그 당시 ("at that time"), but it can also be used directly after a noun to mean "at the time of (noun)." 창립 당시 literally means "at the time of foundation" or "at the time of establishment."

전 is a Sino-Korean word that can be used as an adjective to mean "every," "all," or "whole." For example, 전세계 is a combination of 전 with 세계 ("the world") and means "the whole world."

자발적으로 is an adverb that comes from 자발적 ("voluntary") which can also be used as the descriptive verb 자발적이다 ("to be voluntary").

정기적인 comes from 정기적이다 meaning "to be regular" or "to be periodic."

알려져 있다 comes from 알려지다 meaning "to be (well) known." The conjugated form with 있다 shows that something is in *the state of* being (well) known – here, 알려져 있다 means "to be in the state of being (well) known." A more natural translation for 알려져 있다 could be "it is well known." Since the topic of this sentence is 빌리 건설 ("Billy Construction"), ending the sentence with 참여하고 있는 것으로 is saying that 빌리 건설 is what's in the state of being (well) known for participating.

창립 = "foundation," "establishment"
창립(이) 되다 = "to be founded," "to be established"
당시 = "at that time"
전 = "every," "all"
임직원 = "staff (member)," "employee"
자발적으로 = "voluntarily"
자발적 = "voluntary"
자발적이다 = "to be voluntary"
정기적이다 = "to be regular," "to be periodic"
봉사 = "service," "work"
봉사 활동 = "service project," "volunteer work"

빌리 건설 사랑의 연탄 2만 장 전달

참여(를) 하다 = "to participate," "to take part in"
알려지다 = "to be (well) known"

빌리 건설은 2019 년 사회 활동을 통해 대통령 상을 수상하기도 했다.
"Billy Construction even received the Presidential Award through its social activities in 2019."

Use 통해(서) to show that something happens "through" or "by way of" a noun. Take a noun and attach the Object Marker (을/를), followed by 통해(서) – the 서 is optional.

대통령 상 is a kind of 상 ("award") given by a 대통령 ("president").

The ~기도 하다 form (seen at the end of this sentence) is made by attaching 기도 하다 to the end of a verb stem and then conjugating 하다. It means "to even do (verb)." It's a combination of the standard nominalization ending ~기 together with 도 ("also," "even," "too") and 하다 ("to do"). 수상하기도 하다 means "to even receive (a prize)."

~(을/를) 통해(서) = "through," "by way of"
상 = "prize," "award"
대통령 상 = "Presidential Award"
수상(을) 하다 = "to be awarded," "to receive (a prize)"
~기도 하다 = "to even (verb)"

이번 달 22 일 진행된 사랑의 연탄 봉사 활동에서는 임원들과 가족들이 참여하여 연탄 2 만 장을 서울시 곳곳의 독거노인 및 저소득 가정에 직접 전달했다.
"From the 'Briquettes of Love' service project that went ahead this month on the 22nd, employees and family members participated and personally delivered 20,000 briquettes to senior citizens living alone and low-income families all around the city of Seoul."

및 is a slightly formal-sounding word that means "and." It's used to connect two nouns, and usually only appears in writing. In the example, 독거노인 및 저소득 가정 means "senior citizens living alone *and* low-income families."

진행(이) 되다 = "to progress," "to go along"
서울시 = "the city of Seoul"
곳곳 = "various places," "all around (here and there)"
독거노인 = "senior citizen living alone"
독거 = "living alone," "solitary life"
노인 = "elderly," "senior citizen"
및 = "and"
저소득 = "low-income"
가정 = "family," "household"
저소득 가정 = "low-income family"

빌리 건설 사랑의 연탄 2만 장 전달

빌리 건설은 이달 초에 사랑의 김치 나누기 행사를 개최하였으며 매달 첫째 주 금요일에는 저소득 가정에 사랑의 쌀을 20 포대씩 전달하고 있다.

"Billy Construction held the 'Kimchi of Love' sharing event at the beginning of this month, and on each of the first Fridays of every month is delivering 20 sacks of 'Rice of Love' to low-income families."

이달 means "this month," and 초 means "beginning (part)." To say "the end" of the month use 말, meaning "end (part)," instead of 초. Both 초 and 말 can be used in this same way to say "the beginning" or "the end" with years (년), months (월), and weeks (주).

You can optionally attach ~씩 ("each," "a," "per") after a counter word (here, 포대) to emphasize the meaning of "each." In the example, 20 포대씩 means "20 bags each" – here, 씩 is referring to each time they do the 'Rice of Love' event (not that they give 20 bags of rice to each low-income family).

이달 = "this month"
초 = "beginning (part)"
이달 초 = "the beginning of this month"
말 = "end (part)"
이달 말 = "the end of this month"
나누다 = "to share," "to distribute"
행사 = "event," "ceremony"
개최(를) 하다 = "to hold (a meeting or event)"
매달 = "every month"
첫째 주 = "first week"
포대 = "(burlap) bag," "sack"
~씩 = "each," "a," "per"

이 외에도 빌리 건설의 임직원들은 다양한 사내 봉사활동 동아리를 통해 헌혈 활동, 무료 급식, 노숙인 쉼터 등 다양한 봉사활동에 지속적으로 참여하고 있다.

"In addition, Billy Construction's employees through various in-house service project clubs are continuously participating in blood donation activities, free meal services, homeless shelters, and various service projects."

동아리 means "club" or "group," and is specifically for any sort of group or circle of likeminded people, or people who share the same interests. For example, a school chess club would also be a 동아리.

등 ("and so on," "and others," "etc.") can be attached after a list of items to show that there are more items which aren't listed – this is similar to attaching "et cetera" or "etc." to the end of a list.

이 외에(도) = "in addition (to this/that)"
다양하다 = "to be diverse," "to be various/varied"
사내 = "in-house," "in the company"

빌리 건설 사랑의 연탄 2만 장 전달

동아리 = "club," "group"
헌혈 = "blood donation"
급식 = "(provided) meal," "meal service"
노숙인 = "homeless (person)"
쉼터 = "rest area," "shelter"
노숙인 쉼터 = "homeless shelter"
등 = "and so on," "and others," "etc."
지속적으로 = "continuously," "consistently"

기업 관계자는 '더불어 사는 세상을 통해 많은 사람들의 행복이 건설되길 바란다'며 앞으로도 다양한 공헌 활동을 통해 사랑과 행복을 전달할 것이라고 말했다.

"A company official said 'I hope that many people's happiness can be constructed through a world where we live together,' and said that from now too they will deliver love and happiness through various contribution activities."

관계자 means a person who's directly connected to or concerned with an issue. When talking about a 기업 ("company," "business") 관계자, it's referring to an "official" who's directly connected with the issue at a company – "a person concerned (with)in the company."

더불어 is a slightly formal-sounding adverb that means that two or more people are doing something together or cooperating.

The 며 used after the quote is again the verb ending ~(으)며. It can be attached directly to the end of a verb or a quote ending with the Plain Form (when quoting something that someone says), just like the verb ending~고. You can think of '바란다'며 as being similar to '바란다'고 (말)하고. In the example, 며 is being used as a shortened version of (말)하(며) – here, meaning "(someone) said they hope...."

앞으로도 is a combination of 앞으로 meaning "from now (on)" or "in the future" and the particle 도 ("also," "too," "even"). It's commonly used to express that something will not stop, but will continue on into the future. A more natural translation of "from now on too they will deliver" from the example would be "they will continue delivering."

관계자 = "person(s) concerned," "person(s) connected," "official"
더불어 = "together (with)," "along (with)"
건설(이) 되다 = "to be constructed"

[고빌리 신문 제미 기자 J-gija@gobillykorean.com]

"GoBilly News, Reporter Jemi"

축하드립니다

"코리안 파이팅" 대회

안녕하세요. GoBillyKorean 채널 담당자 빌리입니다.

먼저 2019 년 "코리안 파이팅" 대회에 입상하신 것을 진심으로 축하드립니다.

최우수상 부상으로 한국행 왕복 비행기 표 1 장과 김치 1 통을 전달해 드리기 위해 추가적으로 필요한 정보가 있음을 알려드립니다.

참고로 아래의 정보는 내년 1 월 1 일까지 보관되고 그 이후에는 파기됩니다.

또한 앞서 대회 참가 전에 동의하셨던 대회 규칙도 다시 첨부해서 보내드립니다.

다음 주 금요일 전까지 아래 빈칸의 내용을 기재하시어 보내주시길 바랍니다.

------------------------------------ 아 래 ------------------------------------

성별:
생년월일:
거주 국가:
이메일 주소:
전화번호:

코리안 파이팅 2019 대회 규칙.hwp

"코리안 파이팅" 대회
"'Let's Go Korean' Competition"

파이팅 (also often said as 화이팅) is a common chant when cheering someone on – it can be heard at sports games and is used to encourage friends. Although it originally came from the English word "fighting," it has the meaning of "(Let's) go!" or "Good luck!" or "Come on!"

파이팅! = "(Let's) go!"
대회 = "competition," "tournament"

안녕하세요. GoBillyKorean 채널 담당자 빌리입니다.
"Hello. I'm Billy, and I'm in charge of the channel GoBillyKorean."

Notice how 담당자 comes directly before 빌리 – this reads like "Billy, the person in charge."

채널 = "(TV, etc.) channel"
담당자 = "person in charge"

축하드립니다

먼저 2019 년 "코리안 파이팅" 대회에 입상하신 것을 진심으로 축하드립니다.

"First I'd like to congratulate you from the bottom of my heart on winning the 2019 'Let's Go Korean' Competition."

먼저 means "first," as in you're going to do something first before anything or anyone else.

Use 축하(를) 하다 – here as the humble (and therefore extra polite) version 축하(를) 드리다 – together with a conjugated verb and 것(을) to congratulate someone "on" (or "for") doing something.

먼저 = "first" (adverb)
입상(을) 하다 = "to win (a reward)"
진심으로 = "sincerely," "from the (bottom of someone's) heart"
축하(를) 하다 = "to congratulate"
축하(를) 드리다 = 축하(를) 하다 (humble)

최우수상 부상으로 한국행 왕복 비행기 표 1 장과 김치 1 통을 전달해 드리기 위해 추가적으로 필요한 정보가 있음을 알려드립니다.

"I'm letting you know that there's additional information we need in order to deliver your one round-trip ticket to Korea and one container of kimchi as an additional reward for the grand prize."

최우수상 means "grand prize," but it itself doesn't mean a physical prize or item – 부상 can be added (meaning "an additional prize item") to mean that there's a physical reward.

한국행 combines 한국 ("Korea") with the Sino-Korean word 행 meaning "(going) toward." 행 is used after location names to show that a vehicle is going in that direction.

왕복 is "round-trip," while 편도 is "one-way." For example, 왕복 비행기 표 is "round-trip plane ticket."

통 is a counter used to count containers – 김치 1 통 means "one container of kimchi."

추가적 means "additional," and it can be used with (으)로 to mean "additionally." Alternatively, you can attach 인 (from 이다) to use it as the adjective "additional."

알려드리다 is the humble (and therefore extra polite) form of 알려주다 ("to tell," "to let someone know"). Here it is used together with the verb 있다 ("to exist") changed into a noun with 음/ㅁ as 있음 to mean "to tell (or let someone know) that something exists."

최우수상 = "grand prize"
부상 = "additional prize (item)"
한국행 = "to(ward) Korea"
왕복 = "round-trip"

편도 = "one-way"
비행기 표 = "plane ticket"
통 = container counter
추가적 = "additional"
추가적으로 = "additionally"
추가적이다 = "to be additional"
알려주다 = "to tell," "to let (someone) know"
알려드리다 = 알려주다 (humble)

참고로 아래의 정보는 내년 1 월 1 일까지 보관되고 그 이후에는 파기됩니다.

"For your information, the information below will be kept until next year January 1st, and after that will be destroyed."

참고로 is a common expression in writing (and emails) that means "for reference." It can also be translated as "for your information" or "by the way."

참고로 = "for reference," "for your information," "by the way"
아래 = "the bottom," "below," "under"
보관(이) 되다 = "to be kept," "to be stored"
파기(가) 되다 = "to be destroyed," "to be shredded," "to be broken/cancelled"

또한 앞서 대회 참가 전에 동의하셨던 대회 규칙도 다시 첨부해서 보내드립니다.

"In addition, I'm also attaching the competition rules again which you agreed to previously before entering the competition."

또한 is a formal expression used when adding additional information.

Typically 전에 ("before") and 후에 ("after") are used after verb stems ending with 기 – for example, 참가하기 전에 ("before *participating*") – but they can also be used directly after a noun to mean "before" or "after" that noun. In this sentence 참가 전에 would be like saying "before *participation*." This style of usage is more common in writing.

첨부(를) 하다 means "to attach (something)" and is used for referring to email attachments. 첨부해서 보내다 used here means "to attach and send (something)."

또한 = "also," "in addition"
앞서 = "previously (before now)," "beforehand," "ahead (of)," "earlier"
참가 = "participation," "entry"
동의(를) 하다 = "to agree," "to consent"
규칙 = "rule(s)," "regulation"
첨부(를) 하다 = "to attach (something)," "to add (something)"

축하드립니다

다음 주 금요일 전까지 아래 빈칸의 내용을 기재하시어 보내주시길 바랍니다.

"I hope that you can fill in the contents in the blanks below and send them to me before next Friday."

다음 ("next") is used together with 주 ("week") when referring to the next "day" of a week. 다음 주 금요일 (literally, "next week Friday") translates more naturally to just "next Friday."

빈칸 comes from 비다 ("to be empty," "to be blank") and 칸 ("[marked] space").

까지 ("by," "until") can also be used after 전 ("before") to mean "before (and not after)." Just 금요일까지 means "by Friday" and could possibly also include Friday.

하시어 is a written form of 하셔(서), and has the same meaning.

빈칸 = "blank(s)," "blank space"
기재(를) 하다 = "to write in," "to fill in"
~전까지 = "before (and not after)"

---------------------------------- 아 래 ----------------------------------

"Below."

아래 can also be used to mark the bottom of an email or web page.

성별, 생년월일, 거주 국가, 이메일 주소, 전화번호

"Gender, Birthdate, Country of residence, Email address, Phone number."

생년월일 means "birthdate," and includes the year, month, and date. If your birthday were January 1st 1986 then it would be 1986 년 1 월 1 일.

성별 = "gender," "sex"
생년월일 = "(full) birthdate"
거주 = "residence"
국가 = "nation," "country"
거주 국가 = "country of residence"
이메일 주소 = "email address"
전화번호 = "(tele)phone number"

코리안 파이팅 2019 대회 규칙.hwp

"Let's Go Korean 2019 Competition Rules.hwp"

"Hwp" ("Hangul Word Processor") is a document format used in Korea (similar to Microsoft Word).

빌리 건설 새 프로젝트 진행 건

빌리 건설 새 프로젝트 진행 건

안녕하세요, 빌리 건설 고민우님. 고비코 컨설팅의 나최고입니다.

금번 프로젝트를 본격적으로 진행하기에 앞서 하기 데이터 전달 요청드립니다.

1) 빌리 건설 최근 5 년간 매출표

2) 빌리 나노 건설 기술 공인 기관 인증서

바쁘시겠지만 2 월 22 일 오후 2 시까지 전달해 주시길 부탁드립니다.

감사합니다.

나최고 드림

나최고 팀장
Tel 02-1234-5678
Mobile 010-0001-0002
E-mail best@GBKconsulting.com
Add 서울시 빌리구 키캣로 1 길 11-22 우) 00001

빌리 건설 새 프로젝트 진행 건.

"Billy Construction new project progress case."

Both 새 and 새로운 are adjectives that mean "new," but only 새로운 can be used to mean "new" when talking about people. For items, either can be used.

새 = "new"
진행 = "progress"
건 = "case," "matter"

안녕하세요, 빌리 건설 고민우님. 고비코 컨설팅의 나최고입니다.

"Hello, Mr. Go Min-woo of Billy Construction. This is Na Choi-go of Gobiko Consulting."

님 is a formal title that can be added after a person's name to show extra respect – this is more polite than 씨 ("Mr.," "Mrs.," "Ms.," "Miss"). In addition, 님 can be added after a person's name (or username) on the Internet when speaking politely; for example, you could refer to a person online with the username keykat88 as keykat88 님.

님 = formal title ending
컨설팅 = "consulting"

빌리 건설 새 프로젝트 진행 건

금번 프로젝트를 본격적으로 진행하기에 앞서 하기 데이터 전달 요청드립니다.

"In order to carry on this project for real, I'm requesting beforehand the delivery of the data below."

금번 is a formal word that has the same usage as 이번, meaning "this (time)" or "this occasion." 금번 프로젝트 translates to "this project," but you can also think of it as meaning "the project at hand" or "the current project."

본격적으로 is an adverb that comes from 본격적 ("regular," "real," "full-fledged"), and means to do something "for real" or "in earnest."

~기에 can be attached to the end of an action verb stem to mean "(in order) to" (among other uses), and in this usage it's similar to attaching ~기 위해(서).

The word 하기 in 앞서 하기 means "following" or "under" – in this case, it's referring to the two items listed below.

드리다 is the humble form of 주다 ("to give"), and frequently appears in expressions showing thanks or when asking ("giving") requests; 요청(을) 드리다 is the humble form of 요청(을) 하다.

금번 = "this (time)," "this occasion"
본격적 = "regular," "real," "full-fledged"
본격적으로 = "in earnest," "for real," "full-scale"
진행(을) 하다 = "to progress," "to preside over," "to carry on"
~기에 = "(in order) to"
하기 = "following," "under"
데이터 = "data"
요청(을) 하다 = "to request," "to ask for"
요청(을) 드리다 = 요청(을) 하다 (humble)

빌리 건설 최근 5 년간 매출표

"Billy Construction's sales statements for the most recent 5 years."

최근 = "the latest," "the most recent"
매출 = "sales"
매출표 = "sales statement"

빌리 나노 건설 기술 공인 기관 인증서

"Billy Nano Construction Technology's authorized organization certification."

공인 means "official approval," but when used as an adjective before another noun (with or without adding 의) it can also mean "(officially) authorized." 공인 기관 인증서 is a certificate used in Korea to authorize that an organization has official approval to operate – in this case, whether Billy Nano Construction Technology has authorization.

기술 = "technology," "skill"
공인 = "official approval"
기관 = "organization"
인증서 = "certificate (of authentication)"

바쁘시겠지만 2 월 22 일 오후 2 시까지 전달해 주시길 부탁드립니다.

"You must be busy, but I'm requesting that you deliver this by February 22nd 2 o'clock PM."

부탁(을) 드리다 is the humble form of 부탁(을) 하다, meaning "to request" or "to ask for." However, unlike 요청(을) 드리다 which can be used for either requesting someone to do something or for requesting a necessary item, 부탁(을) 드리다 is used specifically for requesting someone to do something. To say what you're requesting, attach 기(를) – often shortened to 길 – to the end of an action verb stem. 전달해 주시길 부탁(을) 드리다 means "to request to (please) deliver."

부탁(을) 하다 = "to request," "to ask for"
부탁(을) 드리다 = 부탁(을) 하다 (humble)

감사합니다.

"Thank you."

나최고 드림

"From Na Choi-go."

When ending a formal letter, use your name followed by 드림 (meaning you're humbly "giving" them the letter). You may also use 올림 (literally "raising up" the letter) for even more formal letters. When writing letters to friends, instead use your name followed by 이가 (if your name ends in a consonant) or 가 (if your name ends in a vowel). For any other non-formal or casual situation you can also use 씀 ("writing").

드림 = "from" (formal)
올림 = "from" (extra formal)
~(이)가 = "from" (casual)
씀 = "from" (informal)

나최고 팀장

"Team leader Na Choi-go."

팀장 is a combination of 팀 ("team") with 장 ("leader," "head," "chief"), and means the person who's in charge of the team – the "team leader."

팀장 = "team leader"

빌리 건설 새 프로젝트 진행 건

Tel 02-1234-5678

"Telephone number 02-1234-5678."

Obviously 02-1234-5678 is a fake phone number, but it shows the format of a standard telephone in a home or office. The first two or three digits are the area code. Numbers starting with 02 are typically within 서울 or neighboring areas. "Tel" is a written abbreviation of "telephone number."

Mobile 010-0001-0002

"Mobile number 010-0001-0002."

Korean mobile phone numbers start with a three-digit area code. The rest of the digits will have the same format as a standard telephone number.

E-mail best@GBKconsulting.com

The email address best@GBKconsulting.com is a play on words due to the person's name being 나최고 – although a real name, this can also be seen as 나 최고 meaning "I" (나) am "the best" (최고).

Add 서울시 빌리구 키캣로 1 길 11-22 우) 00001

"Address: Seoul City, Billy District, Keykat Road, 1st Street, 11-12, zip code 00001"

"Add" is a written abbreviation of "address."

Addresses in Korea are listed in order from the largest unit to the smallest, with the city going first and the building number (and unit number) going last; the very last number listed is the postal code.

Main streets are named with 로 ("road," "street"), and along those streets can be several smaller streets named with 길 ("street," "road," "way"). 11-12 is the number of the building.

우 is an abbreviation used when writing addresses that means 우편 번호 ("zip code," "postal code").

로 = "road," "street"

우편 번호 = "zip code," "postal code"

한국어의 이해 - 과제 점수 누락 [무역학과 202020212 이영희]

한국어의 이해 - 과제 점수 누락 [무역학과 202021212 이영희]

안녕하세요, 고빌리 교수님.

저는 한국어의 이해를 수강 중인 무역학과 20 학번 이영희입니다.

교수님의 한국어의 이해 수업을 듣고 한국어 공부를 깊이 할 수 있어서 도움이 많이 되고 있습니다.

다름이 아니라 제가 지난주에 제출했던 과제 점수가 누락된 것 같습니다.

교수님께서 쉽게 찾아보실 수 있도록 제출했던 과제를 이메일에 첨부했습니다.

바쁘시겠지만 다시 한번 확인해 주시면 감사하겠습니다.

내일 수업에서 뵙겠습니다. 감사합니다.

이영희 드림.

한국어의 이해_중간 과제_202021212 이영희.hwp

한국어의 이해 - 과제 점수 누락 [무역학과 202021212 이영희]

"Understanding of Korean – Assignment score omission [International Trade Major 202021212 Lee Yung-hee]."

한국어의 이해 is the title of the course – "Understanding of Korean." Currently the student 이영희 is enrolled in the class and is writing an email to her professor about an omitted assignment score.

202021212 is 이영희's student number – it includes the first year she enrolled at the school (2020), along with a unique identification number (21212). The next student who entered after her in the same year would be 202021213.

무역학과 = "international trade (major)"
과제 = "assignment"
점수 = "grade," "score"
누락 = "omission," "leaving out"

안녕하세요, 고빌리 교수님.

"Hello, Professor Go Billy."

When addressing a professor, use 교수님. To talk about "professors" or a professor in general when there's no need to be extra polite (without addressing a specific one), use 교수 instead ("professor").

한국어의 이해 - 과제 점수 누락 [무역학과 202021212 이영희]

교수 = "professor"

교수님 = "professor" (title)

저는 한국어의 이해를 수강 중인 무역학과 20 학번 이영희입니다.

"I'm Lee Yung-hee, started school here in 2020, international trade major, and currently taking 'Understanding of Korean'."

학번 ("student number") can also be used to refer to the last two digits of the year that a student first enrolled at a school - 20 학번 means a student who first started school in 2020.

학번 = "student number"

교수님의 한국어의 이해 수업을 듣고 한국어 공부를 깊이 할 수 있어서 도움이 많이 되고 있습니다.

"I'm taking your 'Understanding of Korean' class, and it's been very helpful because I can study Korean in depth."

Notice how the sentence ends with the ~고 있다 form (수업을 듣고 does not use it) – this form only needs to be used once at the end of a sentence to give the entire sentence the meaning of currently doing something.

깊이 = "deeply," "in depth"

다름이 아니라 제가 지난주에 제출했던 과제 점수가 누락된 것 같습니다.

"The reason I'm emailing you is because I think that the grade for the assignment I submitted last week is missing."

다름이 아니라 comes from 다름 ("something special") and 아니라 ("it isn't, but..."), and literally means "It's nothing special." It's a common phrase used at the beginning of a conversation (in email or on the phone) before discussing the main thing that you want to talk about. Another similar phrase is 다름이 아니고.

다름이 아니라 = "The reason I'm contacting you is...," "for no other reason than"

제출(을) 하다 = "to submit," "to turn in"

누락(이) 되다 = "to be omitted," "to be left out," "to be missing"

교수님께서 쉽게 찾아보실 수 있도록 제출했던 과제를 이메일에 첨부했습니다.

"I've attached to the email the assignment that I submitted so that you can easily find it."

When referring to a person, 찾아보다 can also mean "to go visit" or "to pay (someone) a visit." When referring to an object, it means "to find" or "to search for."

찾아보다 = "to find," "to search for," "to go visit," "to pay (someone) a visit"

한국어의 이해 - 과제 점수 누락 [무역학과 202021212 이영희]

바쁘시겠지만 다시 한번 확인해 주시면 감사하겠습니다.
"You must be busy, but I'd be grateful if you would please check once again."

다시 한번 = "once more," "(once) again," "a second time"
확인(을) 하다 = "to check," "to confirm"

내일 수업에서 뵙겠습니다. 감사합니다.
"I'll see you in class tomorrow. Thank you."

뵙다 is an honorific form of 보다 ("to see"), and slightly more honorific than 뵈다 (which is also an honorific form of 보다). Note that 뵙다 is used when attaching the ~겠다 ending (not 뵈다). Also note that 뵈다 is used with the ~게(요) ending (not 뵙다) – for example, 내일 뵐게요 ("I'll see you tomorrow.").

뵙다 = "to see" (extra humble)
뵈다 = "to see" (humble)

이영희 드림.
"From Lee Yung-hee."

한국어의 이해_중간 과제_202021212 이영희.hwp
"Understanding of Korean_midterm assignment_202021212 Lee Yung-hee.hwp"

When used before another noun, 중간 can mean "midterm."

중간 = "middle," "between," "midterm"

두부

두부가 한 모
깨끗한 두부다
네모난 두부다
단단한 두부다
뚱뚱한 두부다
시원한 두부다
담백한 두부다
나도 두부다

두부
"Tofu"

두부 = "tofu"

두부가 한 모
"One block of tofu."

모 is a counter used for blocks – specifically blocks of tofu.

모 = (tofu) block counter

깨끗한 두부다
"It's clean tofu."

When used in the Plain form, 이다 shortens to just 다 after a vowel.

네모난 두부다
"It's square tofu."

네모(가) 나다 = "to be square (shaped)"

두부

단단한 두부다

"It's firm tofu."

단단하다 = "to be solid," "to be firm"

뚱뚱한 두부다

"It's plump tofu."

While 뚱뚱하다 normally is used to mean "fat," it can also mean that something is plump or bloated. Here it's being used to mean that the tofu is soft and filled with liquid.

뚱뚱하다 = "to be fat," "to be plump"

시원한 두부다

"It's cool tofu."

In many cases 시원하다 is used to refer to hot (and often spicy) soup. However, in this poem it just means "refreshing." The reason that some people might describe hot or spicy soup as 시원하다 is because of the cool feeling they get when sweating while eating it (sweating can cause a cooling feeling).

시원하다 = "to be cool," "to be refreshing"

담백한 두부다

"It's light tofu."

담백하다 means that something tastes light (bland), and not greasy.

담백하다 = "to be light," "to be bland"

나도 두부다

"I'm tofu too."

우리 집 동물

오도도도 산속 다람쥐

아우우우 옆집 강아지

우끼끼끼 정글 침팬지

와다다다 울 집 내 새끼

우리 집 동물
"Our house animal"

오도도도 산속 다람쥐
"Dash! Goes the squirrel far up in a mountain."

오도도도 is a mimetic word (의태어) – onomatopoeia that mimics the sound of something moving or doing something, or mimics a feature of something. 오도도도 is used to mimic the sound of something small (such as a squirrel) running quickly. This is different from regular onomatopoeia (의성어), which mimics the sound that someone or something makes.

산속 is a combination of 산 ("mountain") and 속 ("inside"), and is used to refer to deep (far up) within a mountain area. It doesn't mean the literal inside of a mountain.

의태어 = "mimetic word"
의성어 = "onomatopoeia"
오도도도 = something small running quickly (mimetic word)
산속 = "far up in a mountain"
다람쥐 = "squirrel"

아우우우 옆집 강아지
"Howl! Goes the dog next door."

아우우우 is an onomatopoeia for the sound of an animal howling (just like 아우우우 sounds).

옆집 is a combination of 옆 ("side") and 집 ("house") which means the next door house, or the neighbor's house.

Although 강아지 literally means "puppy," it's also commonly used as a friendly way to refer to any regular "dog."

우리 집 동물

아우우우 = howling (onomatopoeia)
옆집 = "next door (house)," "neighbor (house)"
강아지 = "puppy," "dog"

우끼끼끼 정글 침팬지
"Ooh ooh aah aah! Goes the jungle chimpanzee."

우끼끼끼 is an onomatopoeia for the sound that a small primate such as a monkey makes ("Ooh ooh aah aah!").

우끼끼끼 = primate shout (onomatopoeia)
정글 = "jungle"
침팬지 = "chimpanzee"

와다다다 울 집 내 새끼
"Dash! Goes my kid."

와다다다 is a mimetic word for the sound of something large (such as a person) running quickly.

울 집 is a shortened version of 우리 집 ("our house" or "my house"). It can also be used to mean something of (or from) a certain home.

새끼 ("child") is an informal way to refer to a baby or child. However, this word is also often used as a swear word for insulting someone, so be careful to only use this word in an appropriate context to avoid confusion.

와다다다 = something large running quickly (mimetic word)
울 집 = "our house," "my house" (우리 집)
새끼 = "child" (informal)

밤

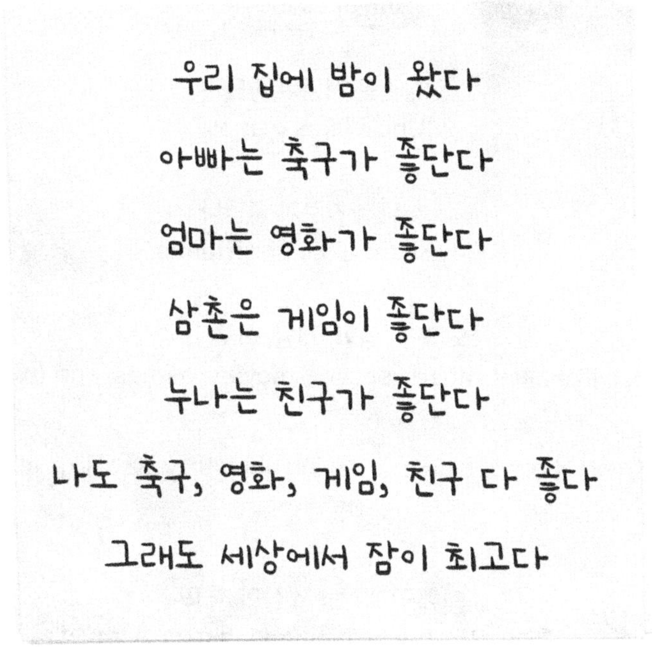

우리 집에 밤이 왔다
아빠는 축구가 좋단다
엄마는 영화가 좋단다
삼촌은 게임이 좋단다
누나는 친구가 좋단다
나도 축구, 영화, 게임, 친구 다 좋다
그래도 세상에서 잠이 최고다

밤
"Nighttime"

Note that 밤 can translate as both "night" and "nighttime" depending on the context.

우리 집에 밤이 왔다
"It's night at our house."

밤(이) 오다 literally means "night comes," and is used to show that the time has changed to become nighttime – as opposed to simply saying that it already is night.

밤(이) 오다 = "night comes"

아빠는 축구가 좋단다
"Dad likes soccer."

축구 means "soccer" if you're American or "football" if you're European.

좋단다 is from the standard quoting form. It's a shortening of 좋다고 (말)한다 – "Dad says he likes soccer." However, the quoting form can also be used simply to report some information – "(someone) says that...." 아빠는 축구가 좋단다 can therefore either be "Dad says he likes soccer" or "They say that (I heard that) dad likes soccer."

축구 = "soccer"

엄마는 영화가 좋단다

"Mom likes movies."

삼촌은 게임이 좋단다

"Uncle likes games."

누나는 친구가 좋단다

"My sister likes her friends."

나도 축구, 영화, 게임, 친구 다 좋다

"I also like all of those - soccer, movies, games, and friends."

다 좋다 means "all are good," so the poet here is saying that they also like all of the things that their family members like.

그래도 세상에서 잠이 최고다

"But still, the best thing in life is sleep."

그래도 can mean "(but) still" or "however" at the start of a sentence, or "though" at the start or middle of a sentence.

잠 comes from the noun form of 자다 ("to sleep") and means "sleep." In fact, the verb 잠(을) 자다 ("to sleep") literally means "to sleep a sleep."

그래도 = "(but) still," "however"
세상에서 = "in the world"
잠 = "sleep"

기린

GBK0909

태어나서 처음 만난 기린. 먹이도 줄수 있어서 좋았다. 손에 아무것도 없는데 주는척 하면 기린이 본척도 안한다. 기다란 목과 혀를 가진 기린과의 눈맞춤과 끈적한 침은 덤.

#동물원 #기린 #속눈썹미인 #혀길다 #여행 #가을 #나도먹고싶다 #맛있니

좋아요 15 개

댓글 10 개

기린

"Giraffe"

기린 = "giraffe"

태어나서 처음 만난 기린.

"The first giraffe I ever met in my life."

기린

먹이도 줄 수 있어서 좋았다.

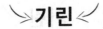

"It was nice because I could give it food too."

Note that the original poster writes 줄수 *incorrectly* without a space. Spacing errors are normal everywhere in Korean, and are especially common online.

The ~서 form is often used together with verbs that show emotion (here with 좋다 meaning "to be good"). Since 좋다 can also be used after a noun with the Subject Marker (이/가) to mean "(I) like...," you could naturally translate 좋았다 in this usage as "I was happy."

먹이 = "(animal) food," "feed"

손에 아무것도 없는데 주는척하면 기린이 본 척도 안 한다.

"If I pretend to give it something but there's nothing in my hand, the giraffe doesn't even pretend to look."

You can use 척하다 after a verb that's been conjugated to an adjective (conjugated to be used directly before a noun). This works with both descriptive verbs and action verbs. Descriptive verbs conjugate as normal to the present tense; 슬픈 척하다 means "to pretend to be sad." When using an action verb, use either the present tense or past tense conjugation – they have the same meaning. 주는 척하다 and 준 척하다 both mean "to pretend to give."

The verb used before 척하다 can either have a space, or be attached directly to 척하다. 주는 척하다 and 주는척하다 are both correct.

Alternatively, you can also use the verb 체하다 in the same way as 척하다. 체하다 is less common.

척하다 = "to pretend," "to act"
체하다 = "to pretend," "to act"

기다란 목과 혀를 가진 기린과의 눈 맞춤과 끈적한 침은 덤.

"Eye contact with a giraffe with a very long neck and tongue, with some slimy spit as a bonus."

When used as an adjective to say that someone or something "has (something)," 가지다 ("to have," "to hold") will become conjugated in the past tense as 가진.

기다랗다 = "to be (very) long"
눈 맞춤 = "eye contact"
끈적하다 = "to be slimy," "to be sticky"
침 = "saliva," "spit"
덤 = "freebie," "extra (thing)"

기린

#동물원 #기린 #속눈썹미인 #혀길다 #여행 #가을 #나도먹고싶다 #맛있니

"#zoo #giraffe #eyelash_beauty #tongue_long #travel #autumn #i_want_to_eat_it_too #does_it_taste_good"

Hashtags in Korea will be whatever is currently popular – trends can change on a weekly or daily basis. Instead of memorizing any of these specific ones here (as they were simply made up for this post), look at whatever social platform you use and take note of what's being used there.

Although 미인 is most often used to mean a beautiful woman, it can also be used for an attractive male.

The ~니 ending (used in #맛있니) has the same meaning as the ~나(요) ending, but is only for casual use. ~니 also has a softer sound than ~나(요).

동물원 = "zoo"
속눈썹 = "eyelash(es)"
미인 = "beauty," "beautiful person"
~니 = (showing curiosity, casual)

좋아요 15 개

"15 likes"

좋아요 (conjugated like this) is what "likes" are called on many social media platforms.

좋아요 = "(social media) like"

댓글 10 개

"10 comments"

댓글 = "(social media) comment"

그림

GBK0909

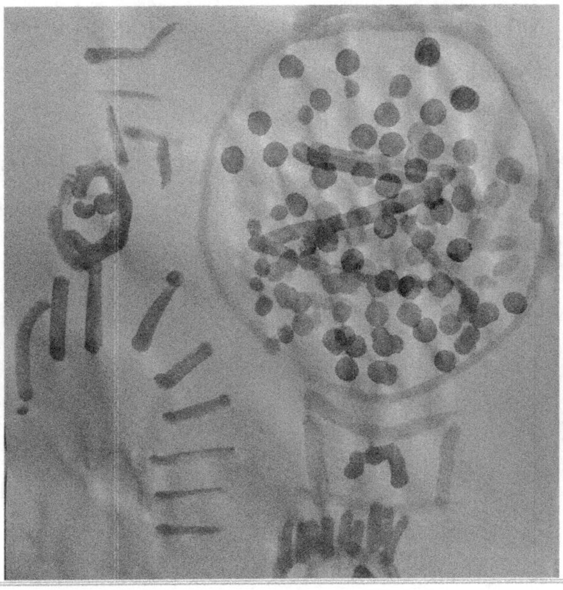

갑자기 그림이 그리고 싶어져서 오랜만에 물감을 꺼내봤다. 예전만큼 잘 그려지지는 않지만 이정도면 만족. 다른 취미생활도 해야하나 싶어서 골프를 쳐봤는데 몸살만 났다. 역시 나는 미술을 해야하나보다.

#취미생활 #예술하는남자 #미술 #페인팅 #감성 #아티스트

좋아요 8 개

댓글 4 개

그림
"Drawing"

갑자기 그림이 그리고 싶어져서 오랜만에 물감을 꺼내봤다.
"I suddenly wanted to draw a drawing so I took out my paints for the first time in a long time."

그림

The ~고 싶다 form added to action verbs can be used as either an action verb, or as a descriptive verb. Therefore, both 그림(을) 그리고 싶다 and 그림(이) 그리고 싶다 are correct and common – this is possible because although 그리다 ("to draw") is only an action verb, 싶다 is a descriptive verb.

싶어져서 comes from 싶어지다 and the ~서 ending. 싶어지다 comes from 싶다 and the ~지다 ending, which can be added after a descriptive verb to mean "to become (descriptive verb)." Using the ~고 싶다 form ("to want to do") as ~고 싶어지다 means that you or someone else literally *becomes* "wanting to do something" that they didn't want to do before.

그림(을) 그리다 = "to draw (a drawing)," "to paint (a picture)"
~지다 = "to become (descriptive verb)"
물감 = "paint (for painting)"

예전만큼 잘 그려지지는 않지만 이 정도면 만족.
"I couldn't draw it as well as I used to, but I'm satisfied with this much."

예전 is used to refer to something that happened a long time ago in the past, but not something that happened in "the old days" or to talk about back when you (as an older person) were just a little kid – for that, instead use 옛날 ("the old days").

만큼 ("as much as," "amount") is used to talk about an amount and is attached directly after a noun (or verb conjugated to an adjective). In the example, 예전만큼 means "as much as the past" or just "as well as I used to."

그려지다 ("to be drawn") is the passive form of 그리다 ("to draw"). Literally, 잘 그려지지 않다 means "to not be drawn well." Since the passive voice in Korean is also used to mean "can" and "can't," 잘 그려지지 않다 is used here to mean "can't draw (it) well."

정도 ("about," "approximately") is often used with 이 ("this") and the verb 되다; for example, 이 정도면 돼요 literally means "If it's about this it's acceptable," or more naturally "This (much) is enough." 만족 ("satisfaction") is used here in place of 되다 to mean "I'm satisfied if it's this (much)" or just "I'm happy with this."

예전 = "the past," "a long time ago"
옛날 = "the old days"
~만큼 = "as much as," "amount"
만족 = "satisfaction"

다른 취미생활도 해야 하나 싶어서 골프를 쳐봤는데 몸살만 났다.
"I wondered if I should have other hobbies too so I tried playing golf, but I only got exhausted and sick."

취미생활 = "(life) having hobbies," "(life) enjoying hobbies"

골프(를) 치다 = "to play golf"
몸살 = "(whole body) sickness (from exhaustion)"
몸살(이) 나다 = "to get sick (from exhaustion)"

역시 나는 미술을 해야 하나 보다.
"I guess I should do art after all."

The ~나 보다 ending is used for saying that you "guess" or that something "seems like" something. In the example, 해야 하나 보다 means "I guess I have to..." or "It seems like I have to...." While most often conjugated, 보다 can also be left as 보다 in casual speech (such as when talking to yourself).

미술 = "art," "fine art," "painting," "drawing"
~나 보다 = "to guess that," "something seems like"

#취미생활 #예술하는남자 #미술 #페인팅 #감성 #아티스트
"#enjoying_hobbies #man_who_does_art #art #painting #sensitivity #artist"

예술 = "art (in general)"
페인팅 = "painting"
감성 = "sense," "sensitivity"
아티스트 = "artist"

좋아요 8 개
"8 likes"

댓글 4 개
"4 comments"

피자

GBK0909

오븐 사고서 처음으로 집에서 만든 피자. 넉넉한 소스와 토핑만 있으면 우리집도 피자 맛집. 오븐에서 꺼내자마자 다 먹었는데 또 생각나는 맛이었다. 이정도면 피자집 안가도 될듯.

#피자 #쿠킹 #우리집 #피자는페퍼로니 #치즈듬뿍 #피자맛집 #피망도넣었어요 #요리하는남자

좋아요 9 개

댓글 5 개

피자

"Pizza"

오븐 사고서 처음으로 집에서 만든 피자.

"The first pizza I made at home after buying an oven."

사고서 is a combination of 사다 ("to buy") with the ~고 나서 ending (often shortened to ~고서), which is used with action verbs to mean "and then" or "after (doing)" to emphasize that something happens after something else.

피자

오븐 = "oven"

넉넉한 소스와 토핑만 있으면 우리 집도 피자 맛집.

"If there's only plenty of sauce and toppings then even our house is a popular pizza restaurant."

만 있으면 literally means "if there is only," but here in the example it would translate more naturally as "if there's (plenty of sauce and toppings)" or "all I need is (plenty of sauce and toppings)."

맛집 is a combination of 맛 ("flavor," "taste") with 집 ("house"); 집 can also be used to mean a "place" when referring to a restaurant. 맛집 therefore literally means "a flavorful place." This term is commonly used both online and offline to refer to any restaurant, or even store (such as a clothing store) that's popular and of high quality. Therefore, you can think of 피자 맛집 as meaning "a place with good pizza."

넉넉하다 = "to be sufficient," "to be plenty," "to be enough"
소스 = "sauce"
토핑 = "topping"
집 = "house," "home," "place (restaurant)"
맛집 = "good place (for food)," "popular store"

오븐에서 꺼내자마자 다 먹었는데 또 생각나는 맛이었다.

"I ate it all as soon as I took it out from the oven, and it was a taste that I'll think about again."

The ~자마자 ending can be attached to an action verb stem to mean "as soon as" that verb happens.

또 생각이 나는 맛 literally means "a flavor that will come (to mind) again," and it means that the writer knows they will remember that taste again later. Using 생각(이) 나다 instead of 생각(을) 하다 adds emphasis to the thing that you will remember.

~자마자 = "as soon as"
생각(이) 나다 = "to come to mind," "to be remembered"

이 정도면 피자집 안 가도 될 듯.

"This seems to be enough that it's okay to not go to a pizza parlor."

~듯 can be added to the end of a verb conjugated to an adjective in any tense (here 되다 becomes the adjective 될 which is in the future tense) to show that something seems "as if" or "as though." Optionally ~듯 can become ~듯이 – both forms are common. When not followed by another verb or sentence, ~듯 can also end with 하다 to mean "to do (verb) as if/though...."

A more natural translation for the example sentence could be "This seems good enough that I don't need to go to a pizza parlor."

피자

피자집 = "pizza parlor," "pizza restaurant"
~듯 = "(seems) as if," "(seems) as though"

#피자 #쿠킹 #우리집 #피자는페퍼로니 #치즈듬뿍 #피자맛집 #피망도넣었어요 #요리하는남자
"#pizza #cooking #our_house #pepperoni_on_pizza #full_of_cheese #popular_pizza_place #i_put_bell_peppers_too #man_who_cooks"

The Topic Marker (은/는) can also be used to state "when it comes to..." or "as for...." Therefore, the hashtag #피자는페퍼로니 (피자는 페퍼로니) could naturally translate as "When it comes to pizza, pepperoni is best" or just "Pepperoni on pizza."

듬뿍 is an adverb that means something is so full or piled up so much that it's going to overflow.

쿠킹 = "cooking"
페퍼로니 = "pepperoni"
듬뿍 = "full," "heaping" "generously"
피망 = "bell pepper"

좋아요 9 개
"9 likes"

댓글 5 개
"5 comments"

임금님 귀는 당나귀 귀

옛날 어느 한 나라에 당나귀 귀처럼 큰 귀를 가진 임금님이 살았습니다. 그 임금님은 항상 커다란 모자를 쓰고 다녔습니다. 임금님은 자신의 귀가 크다는 것을 아무에게도 알리고 싶지 않았습니다. 하지만 임금님의 모자 장인만은 그 비밀을 알고 있었지요. 모자 장인은 이 엄청난 비밀을 누구에게도 말할 수 없어서 너무 답답했습니다. 모자 장인은 한참 동안 이 비밀을 누구에게도 말하지 못해서 가슴이 답답해지고 죽을병에 걸린 것처럼 아파졌습니다. 결국 모자 장인은 사람들이 잘 찾아오지 않는 대나무 숲에 들어가 임금님의 비밀을 큰소리로 외쳤습니다. "임금님 귀는 당나귀 귀! 임금님 귀는 당나귀 귀!" 그러고 나니 모자 장인의 마음은 가벼워지고 병도 모두 나았지요. 그런데 그 뒤로 바람이 불면 대나무 숲에서 "임금님 귀는 당나귀 귀" 하는 소리가 들려왔습니다. 소문을 들은 임금님은 그 대나무 숲의 대나무를 모두 베어버리게 했습니다. 하지만 대나무가 남지 않은 숲에서도 여전히 "임금님 귀는 당나귀 귀" 하는 메아리가 들려왔습니다. 충격과 부끄러움으로 병을 얻은 임금님은 시름시름 앓았습니다. 그러다가 임금님은 한 점쟁이에게 큰 귀는 좋은 관상이라는 이야기를 듣게 됩니다. 임금님은 그 이야기에 힘을 얻고 일어났습니다. 그리고 백성들에게 당당하게 귀를 보이며 "앞으로 이 큰 귀로 백성들의 이야기를 열심히 듣겠다" 라고 말했지요. 그 임금님은 오래오래 태평성대를 이루며 성군으로 칭송을 받았다고 합니다.

임금님 귀는 당나귀 귀

"The king's ears are donkey ears."

This story as well as the two that follow are traditional folk tales (called 전래 동화). Although this story and many others you will find were actually not originally written in Korea, they have been passed through many countries (including Korea) in various versions throughout history.

While 임금 means "king" or "ruler," using 임금님 here shows respect toward that person; it's common to add 님 to titles to show respect.

임금 = "king," "ruler"
임금님 = "king," "ruler" (honorific)
당나귀 = "donkey"
전래 동화 = "traditional folk tale"

임금님 귀는 당나귀 귀

옛날 어느 한 나라에 당나귀 귀처럼 큰 귀를 가진 임금님이 살았습니다.

"A long time ago in a country lived a king who had big ears like donkey's ears."

어느 typically means "what kind of" or "what type of" when used in a question, but in a statement it can also mean "a (certain)" or "some" – in the example, 어느 한 나라 literally means "a certain one country" or "some (one) country." It's used often when talking about something (or someone) without specifying any details about which thing it is.

어느 = "a (certain)," "some"

그 임금님은 항상 커다란 모자를 쓰고 다녔습니다.

"The king always wore a huge hat."

쓰고 다니다 literally means "to wear (on one's head) and commute (somewhere)." This means that he wore the hat wherever he went (commuted). Another possible translation of 쓰고 다니다 could be "to wear around." Remember that since 쓰다 is only used for wearing objects on one's head, you can use a different verb together with 다니다 in this same way for doing other actions (입다, etc.).

커다랗다 = "to be (very) big"

임금님은 자신의 귀가 크다는 것을 아무에게도 알리고 싶지 않았습니다.

"The king didn't want to tell anyone that his ears were big."

자신 means "oneself," and in the example refers to the king – literally, "the king himself." 자신 is commonly used when referring to someone in the third person. When used to mean "oneself," another similar word is 자기 ("oneself"). 자기 is more commonly used in casual speech while 자신 is more common in writing and formal speech.

The grammar used at the end of 귀가 크다는 것을 means "that (his ears are big)" or "the fact that (his ears are big)." To use it, take the Plain Form and attach ~는 것(을). This is also used frequently when saying that you or someone knows or doesn't know about something (when followed by 알다 or 모르다), meaning "to know (or not know) that...."

알리다 is originally the causative verb form of 알다 ("to know").

자신 = "oneself"
자신의 = "one's own"
자기 = "oneself"
~는 것(을) = "that (verb)," "the fact that (verb)"
알리다 = "to let (someone) know," "to tell," "to inform"

하지만 임금님의 모자 장인만은 그 비밀을 알고 있었지요.
"But only the king's hat maker knew that secret."

~지요 is the same verb ending as ~죠, but ~죠 is more commonly used in speech while ~지요 is used in writing.

장인 = "(master) artisan," "(skilled) craftsman"
~지요 = ~죠

모자 장인은 이 엄청난 비밀을 누구에게도 말할 수 없어서 너무 답답했습니다.
"Because the hat maker couldn't tell this huge secret to anyone, he was too frustrated."

답답하다 has several uses. In addition to meaning "frustrated" or "irritated" because of something, it can also mean that you feel "stuffy" in a small or poorly ventilated room. Or it can mean that you feel emotionally "heavy" from worrying too much, such as in this sentence.

엄청나다 = "to be tremendous," "to be incredible"
답답하다 = "to be frustrated," "to be irritated," "to feel (emotionally) heavy"

모자 장인은 한참 동안 이 비밀을 누구에게도 말하지 못해서 가슴이 답답해지고 죽을병에 걸린 것처럼 아파졌습니다.
"Because the hat maker couldn't say this secret to anyone for a long time, his chest became heavy and he became sick as if he had a terminal illness."

죽을병 literally means a "disease" (병) that someone "will die" (죽을) from.

한참 = "a long time," "some time"
한참 동안 = "for a long time," "for quite some time"
병 = "disease," "illness"
죽을병 = "fatal disease," "terminal illness"

결국 모자 장인은 사람들이 잘 찾아오지 않는 대나무 숲에 들어가 임금님의 비밀을 큰소리로 외쳤습니다.
"In the end the hat maker went into a bamboo forest that people don't often visit and shouted the king's secret out loud."

In addition to meaning "well," the adverb 잘 can also be used to mean "often."

찾아오다 is the 오다 ("to come") version of 찾아가다 which means "to (go and) visit" or "to drop by" somewhere. These words come from a combination of the verb 찾다 ("to look for," "to find") with 오다 and 가다.

임금님 귀는 당나귀 귀

결국 = "in the end," "ultimately"
잘 = "well," "often"
찾아오다 = "to (come and) visit," "to drop by"
찾아가다 = "to (go and) visit," "to drop by"
대나무 = "bamboo"
숲 = "forest," "grove"
큰소리로 = "out loud," "with a loud voice"
외치다 = "to shout," "to exclaim"

"임금님 귀는 당나귀 귀! 임금님 귀는 당나귀 귀!"
"'The king's ears are donkey ears! The king's ears are donkey ears!'"

그러고 나니 모자 장인의 마음은 가벼워지고 병도 모두 나았지요.
"After that, his heart became light and all of his illnesses were healed."

그러고 나니 has a similar meaning as 그러고 나서, and means "after (doing) that" or "next" after doing something. However, the ~고 나니 ending differs in that it shows something unexpected happened to the speaker. In daily speech, ~고 나니까 is also commonly used.

Saying that his heart became light (마음은 가벼워지고) means that he felt his burden was lifted. You can use 가볍다 ("to be light") and 무겁다 ("to be heavy") with 마음 ("heart," "mind") when talking about whether you feel burdened with something.

그러고 나니(까) = "after (doing) that," "next" (unexpectedly)
~고 나니(까) = "and then," "after (doing)" (unexpectedly)
모두 = "all," "everyone," "everything"
낫다 = "to recover," "to heal"

그런데 그 뒤로 바람이 불면 대나무 숲에서 "임금님 귀는 당나귀 귀" 하는 소리가 들려왔습니다.
"But afterward when the wind blew, you could hear a voice in the bamboo forest saying, 'The king's ears are donkey ears.'"

들려오다 is similar to 들리다 ("to be audible," "to be heard"), but is specifically used for rumors or sounds (or echoes) that reach your ears. It comes from a combination of 들리다 and 오다 ("to come").

그 뒤로 = "afterward," "since then"
들려오다 = "to be heard (here)," "to reach (one's) ears"

소문을 들은 임금님은 그 대나무 숲의 대나무를 모두 베어버리게 했습니다.

"The king who heard the rumor had all of the bamboo in the bamboo forest cut down."

베다 is used for cutting down trees, or cutting things in general. Also 베다 should be used when cutting into something, such as if you cut your finger while cooking – using 자르다 ("to cut") in that situation would mean that you cut off your entire finger.

소문 = "rumor," "gossip"
베다 = "to chop," "to cut"

하지만 대나무가 남지 않은 숲에서도 여전히 "임금님 귀는 당나귀 귀" 하는 메아리가 들려왔습니다.

"But even in the forest where no bamboo remained, you could still hear an echo saying, 'The king's ears are donkey ears!'"

여전히 = "as usual," "as ever," "still"
메아리 = "echo"

충격과 부끄러움으로 병을 얻은 임금님은 시름시름 앓았습니다.

"The king, who got an illness from shock and embarrassment, was sick for a long time."

시름시름 means "lingeringly," and is used together with 앓다 to mean that someone suffers for a long time from a sickness that doesn't quickly go away. Typically 앓다 is used following the Object Marker (을/를) – for example, 병을 앓다.

충격 = "shock"
부끄러움 = "embarrassment," "shame"
앓다 = "to suffer (from an illness)"
시름시름 앓다 = "to suffer (from an illness) for a long time"

그러다가 임금님은 한 점쟁이에게 큰 귀는 좋은 관상이라는 이야기를 듣게 됩니다.

"And then one day the king came to hear from a fortune-teller that big ears were good luck."

그러다가 does not only mean "and then (one day)," but this can be a natural translation at the start of a sentence. It comes from the verb 그러다 ("to say so," "to do so"). The ~다가 ending shows that something interrupts the action verb before it. Therefore, 그러다가 here literally means, "while doing so... (he was interrupted by)...."

이야기 (more often said as 얘기 in everyday speech) literally means "story" or "conversation." Here, 좋은 관상이라는 이야기 is 좋은 관상이라고 (말)하는 이야기, or "a story/conversation that (says) it is good luck." 이야기 can be used in this way to simply talk about something that someone said in a conversation. Here, the king likely had a conversation with a fortune-teller who told him that having big ears were good luck.

임금님 귀는 당나귀 귀

관상 ("physiognomy") is the fortune of a person's character judged from looking at their face. 좋은 관상 therefore means "good fortune," although "good luck" might also be a natural translation.

그러다가 = "and then (one day)"
점쟁이 = "fortune-teller"
관상 = "fortune (from looking at someone's face)"

임금님은 그 이야기에 힘을 얻고 일어났습니다.
"The king took heart from that, and got up."

힘(을) 얻다 literally means "to receive strength," and it's used to mean that someone receives or feels encouragement.

힘(을) 얻다 = "to take heart," "to be encouraged"

그리고 백성들에게 당당하게 귀를 보이며 "앞으로 이 큰 귀로 백성들의 이야기를 열심히 듣겠다" 라고 말했지요.
"And while showing his ears proudly to the people, he said, 'From now on I will listen intently to the people with these big ears.'"

백성 = "the people," "the public"
당당하다 = "to be confident," "to be dignified," "to be proud"
열심히 = "intently," "diligently"
열심히 듣다 = "to be all ears," "to listen intently"

그 임금님은 오래오래 태평성대를 이루며 성군으로 칭송을 받았다고 합니다.
"The king forever reigned peacefully, and received admiration as a great and wise king."

The ending 받았다고 합니다 is a quoting form. Although nobody in the story is directly quoting anything here, finishing a story with a quoting form is similar to adding "and that's how the story goes."

오래오래 = "forever," "for a very long time"
태평성대 = "reign of peace"
이루다 = "to make," "to attain," "to fulfill"
성군 = "great and wise king"
칭송 = "praise," "admiration"

젊어지는 샘물

옛날 어느 마을에 착한 노부부가 살고 있었어요. 할아버지와 할머니는 오랫동안 자식이 생기지 않는 것이 걱정이었어요. 평소처럼 할아버지가 산에서 도끼로 나무를 베고 있는데 갑자기 할아버지 앞에 새가 한 마리 나타났어요. 그 새는 노래하며 할아버지 주위를 맴돌았어요. '이 새가 나한테 따라오라고 하는구나' 라고 생각한 할아버지는 새를 따라서 작은 샘물이 있는 곳에 도착했어요. 목이 말랐던 할아버지는 샘물을 마시고 다시 일어났어요. 그런데 무겁던 도끼가 가볍게 느껴지고 아프던 무릎도 멀쩡하게 느껴졌어요. 놀란 할아버지가 샘물을 들여다보니 젊은 남자의 얼굴이 보였어요. 할아버지는 깜짝 놀라 한걸음에 집으로 돌아왔어요. 할아버지는 자신을 믿지 못하는 할머니를 데리고 샘물을 다시 찾아갔어요. 그리고 샘물을 마신 할머니도 할아버지처럼 젊어졌답니다. 착한 노부부가 젊어졌다는 것을 눈치챈 옆집의 욕심쟁이 할아버지는 두 사람을 찾아와 비결을 알려달라고 졸랐어요. 부부에게 샘물에 대한 이야기를 들은 욕심쟁이 할아버지는 곧장 샘물을 찾아갔어요. 욕심쟁이 할아버지는 옆집 부부보다 더 젊어지고 싶은 욕심에 물을 잔뜩 떠서 허겁지겁 마셨어요. 시간이 한참 지나도 옆집 할아버지가 돌아오지 않는 것이 걱정된 부부는 샘물이 있는 곳으로 찾아갔어요. 옆집 할아버지의 옷 사이에서 울고 있는 아기를 발견한 부부는 아이를 데리고 돌아와 정성스럽게 돌봤어요. 착한 부부의 아들로 자란 아이는 마을에서 유명한 효자가 되었답니다.

젊어지는 샘물

"Spring water of youth."

젊어지다 literally means "to become young" from 젊다 ("to be young," "to be youthful"). Literally 젊어지는 샘물 is "the spring water that (someone) becomes young," but it means that someone who drinks the spring water will become young.

젊다 = "to be young," "to be youthful"
샘물 = "spring water"

옛날 어느 마을에 착한 노부부가 살고 있었어요.

"Long ago in a village there lived a kind elderly couple."

젊어지는 샘물

마을 = "village," "town"
착하다 = "to be good-natured," "to be kindhearted"
부부 = "(married) couple," "husband and wife"
노부부 = "elderly couple," "old couple"

할아버지와 할머니는 오랫동안 자식이 생기지 않는 것이 걱정이었어요.
"The old man and woman were worried for a long time about not having any children."

Although 할아버지 and 할머니 often translate as "grandfather" and "grandmother," they're also used just to refer to anyone of old age (anyone of similar age to a grandfather or grandmother). These terms are still considered respectful.

생기다 means that something new forms which wasn't there before, and it's used in the example to mean "to have" children (becoming pregnant) – literally, 자식이 생기지 않다 means "children are not forming."

걱정 ("worry," "concern") is often used as a verb with 하다 – 걱정(을) 하다 means "to worry." 걱정 can also be used together with the verb 이다 ("to be"), literally meaning "to be a worry." In this sentence it's used with 생기지 않는 것, a noun form of 생기지 않다 ("to not occur," "to not be formed"), and literally means "the not forming (of children) was a worry."

자식 = "child(ren)," "offspring"
생기다 = "to occur," "to be formed"
걱정 = "worry," "concern"
걱정이다 = "to be a worry," "to be worried about"

평소처럼 할아버지가 산에서 도끼로 나무를 베고 있는데 갑자기 할아버지 앞에 새가 한 마리 나타났어요.
"As usual the old man was cutting trees with an axe at the mountain, when suddenly one bird appeared in front of him."

평소 = "usual," "ordinary"
평소처럼 = "as usual," "as ordinary"
도끼 = "axe"
나타나다 = "to appear," "to show up"

그 새는 노래하며 할아버지 주위를 맴돌았어요.
"While the bird sang, it circled around where the old man was."

노래하며 is the same meaning as 노래하면서 – "while singing (a song)."

주위 = "surrounding (area)," "around (somewhere)"
맴돌다 = "to circle (an area)"

젊어지는 샘물

'이 새가 나한테 따라오라고 하는구나' 라고 생각한 할아버지는 새를 따라서 작은 샘물이 있는 곳에 도착했어요.

"The old man thought, 'This bird is telling me to follow it,' and following the bird the old man arrived at a place with a small spring."

따라오다 is a combination of 따르다 ("to follow") and 오다 ("to come"), and means to follow someone or something here. Its opposite is 따라가다 from 따르다 and 가다 ("to go"), meaning to follow someone or something to somewhere else.

Single and double quotes have different uses in Korean. Double quotes are mostly used for quoting what someone *says*, while single quotes are mostly used for quoting what someone *thinks*.

따라오다 = "to (come) follow"
따라가다 = "to (go) follow"

목이 말랐던 할아버지는 샘물을 마시고 다시 일어났어요.

"The old man who was thirsty drank the spring water and stood up again."

You can attach ~던 to a past tense descriptive verb stem (here, 마르다 becoming 말랐던) to make the descriptive verb into a past tense adjective – meaning, in order to conjugate a descriptive verb to describe something in the past tense which is no longer that way. For example, 목이 마른 할아버지 means "old man who is thirsty" and 목이 말랐던 할아버지 means "old man who was thirsty." This is different from using ~던 with action verb stems, which is explained in the journal entry "엄마랑 데이트."

목(이) 마르다 = "to be thirsty"
일어나다 = "to stand up," "to get up"

그런데 무겁던 도끼가 가볍게 느껴지고 아프던 무릎도 멀쩡하게 느껴졌어요.

"But his axe that was heavy felt light, and his knee that was hurt also felt fine."

느껴지다 ("to be felt") is the passive form of 느끼다 ("to feel"), and when used together with a descriptive verb (here, 가볍게) means "to feel (descriptive verb)." Note that 느껴지다 is only used in this way when describing how something feels; to say that you feel (descriptive verb), simply conjugate the descriptive verb as usual. For example, to say that you feel cold simply say 추워요. This applies to both the 1st person ("I," "me") and the 2nd person ("you").

You can (sometimes) also add ~던 to a descriptive verb stem in the regular present tense (here, 무겁던 and 아프던). The difference is that using only ~던 with a descriptive verb stem (instead of ~ㅆ던) means that something was a certain way all the way up to the present – here, 무겁던 means that the axe was heavy continually all the way until right now. This ~던 usage is much less common than the normal ~ㅆ던 ending for descriptive verb stems.

멀쩡하다 means that something is free of defects, damage, disorder, or sickness. A natural translation is "to be fine" or "to be okay." This is slightly different from 괜찮다, which means that something is acceptable to you or all right.

젊어지는 샘물

느껴지다 = "to be felt," "to feel"
무릎 = "knee," "lap"
멀쩡하다 = "to be fine," "to be okay," "to be unhurt"

놀란 할아버지가 샘물을 들여다보니 젊은 남자의 얼굴이 보였어요.
"The surprised old man looked into the spring water, and could see a young man's face."

놀라다 = "to be surprised," "to be amazed"
들여다보다 = "to look in(to)"

할아버지는 깜짝 놀라 한걸음에 집으로 돌아왔어요.
"The old man was startled, and came back home without stopping."

깜짝 놀라다 = "to be startled," "to be very surprised"
한걸음에 = "without stopping," "without (taking) a break"

할아버지는 자신을 믿지 못하는 할머니를 데리고 샘물을 다시 찾아갔어요.
"The old man brought the old woman, who couldn't believe him, and went to visit the spring water again."

그리고 샘물을 마신 할머니도 할아버지처럼 젊어졌답니다.
"And the old lady who drank the spring water also became young like the old man."

젊어졌답니다 is a shortened version of 젊어졌다고 합니다 – the standard quoting form that's often used after telling a story. Using the quoting form in a story is similar to saying "and what happened is...."

착한 노부부가 젊어졌다는 것을 눈치챈 옆집의 욕심쟁이 할아버지는 두 사람을 찾아와 비결을 알려달라고 졸랐어요.
"The greedy old man next door, who noticed that the nice old couple became young, came to visit the two (people) and nagged them to tell him their secret."

비결 means a secret method for doing something (for a regular secret, use 비밀). In the example, the greedy old man wants to know their secret about how they became young.

주다 ("to give") becomes 달라고 whenever the person asking for something is also the person receiving it – just like saying "give me." If the person asking is different from the person receiving something, use 주라고 instead – "give (someone else)." 알려달라고 therefore means "tell me," while 알려주라고 would mean "tell (someone else)."

눈치(를) 채다 = "to notice," "to sense"
욕심쟁이 = "greedy person"
비결 = "secret (method)"
조르다 = "to nag," "to pester"

젊어지는 샘물

부부에게 샘물에 대한 이야기를 들은 욕심쟁이 할아버지는 곧장 샘물을 찾아갔어요.

"The greedy old man who heard from the couple the story about the spring water went straight to visit the spring water."

부부에게 here means "from the couple," together with 듣다 ("to hear") – the old man heard about it "from the couple."

곧장 = "right (away)," "straight"

욕심쟁이 할아버지는 옆집 부부보다 더 젊어지고 싶은 욕심에 물을 잔뜩 떠서 허겁지겁 마셨어요.

"The greedy old man, in his greed of wanting to become younger than the next door couple, scooped out his fill of water and drank it in a hurry."

욕심에 means "in greed," and what comes before it (옆집 부부보다 더 젊어지고 싶은) describes the kind of greed.

욕심 = "greed"
잔뜩 = "to one's fill," "filled"
뜨다 = "to scoop (up)," "to scoop (out)"
허겁지겁 = "in a rush," "hastily"

시간이 한참 지나도 옆집 할아버지가 돌아오지 않는 것이 걱정된 부부는 샘물이 있는 곳으로 찾아갔어요.

"The couple, who became worried at the old man next door not coming back even after a long time had passed, went to visit the place with the spring water."

시간이 한참 지나다 means "time passes for a long time," or "a lot of time goes by."

걱정(이) 되다, which comes from 걱정 ("worry," "concern") and 되다 ("to become"), literally means "to become a worry." It's used to say that someone worries about something that they weren't worried about before.

지나다 = "to pass," "to go by"
시간(이) 지나다 = "time passes," "time goes by"
걱정(이) 되다 = "to become a worry," "to grow uneasy"

옆집 할아버지의 옷 사이에서 울고 있는 아기를 발견한 부부는 아이를 데리고 돌아와 정성스럽게 돌봤어요.

"The couple, who spotted a crying baby between the clothes of the old man next door, took the baby and went back, and looked after him with care."

사이 means the space between something – here, it means the old man's clothes. 사이에서 shows that some action is happening there, between (within) his clothes.

사이 = "space (between)"
발견(을) 하다 = "to discover," "to spot"
정성스럽다 = "to be sincere," "to be careful and respectful"
돌보다 = "to take care of," "to look after"

착한 부부의 아들로 자란 아이는 마을에서 유명한 효자가 되었답니다.
"The baby who was raised as the kind couple's son became a famous devoted son in the village."

효자 is a son who obeys and is dutiful toward his parents. A daughter who's dutiful toward her parents is called 효녀.

자라다 = "to grow (up)," "to be raised"
효자 = "obedient (devoted) son"
효녀 = "obedient (devoted) daughter"

훈장님의 꿀단지

옛날 옛적 작은 마을에 훈장님이 한 명 살고 있었습니다. 그 훈장님은 아이들이 열심히 책을 읽고 있을 때 아이들 몰래 꿀을 꺼내서 먹곤 했습니다. 눈치가 빠른 아이 하나가 그 모습을 발견하고 훈장님에게 물었습니다. "훈장님 저희에게는 엿가락 하나도 나눠 먹으라고 가르치시고 혼자 꿀을 드십니까?" 그 말을 들은 훈장님은 "이건 꿀이 아니라 약이다. 아이들은 먹으면 죽는 약이야." 라고 거짓말을 했습니다. 하루는 훈장님이 아이들에게 책을 읽도록 시키고 잠시 외출을 했습니다. "우리 꿀 한입씩만 먹을까?" 라고 한 아이가 말했습니다. 아이들이 한입씩 꿀을 먹다 보니 꿀단지는 금세 텅 비고 말았습니다. 훈장님에게 혼이 날 생각을 하니 아이들은 걱정이 되었습니다. 그때 똑똑한 아이 하나가 다른 아이들에게 바닥에 누워있으라고 말하고 훈장님이 아끼는 벼루를 마당에 던져 깨뜨렸습니다. 훈장님의 기침 소리가 들리기 시작하자 똑똑한 아이가 마당에 앉아 울기 시작했습니다. 놀라서 달려온 훈장님은 울고 있는 아이 옆에 깨진 벼루와 텅 빈 꿀단지를 보고 입을 다물 수가 없었습니다. "훈장님 저희가 실수로 훈장님께서 아끼시는 벼루를 깼습니다. 그래서 훈장님의 약을 먹고 죽으려고 동무들과 약을 모두 먹었습니다." 그 이야기를 들은 훈장님은 아이들을 차마 혼내지 못하고 집으로 돌려보냈습니다. 그 뒤에 훈장님은 아이들에게 거짓말을 한 것을 사과하고 아이들 몰래 꿀을 먹던 버릇을 고쳤다고 합니다.

훈장님의 꿀단지

"The village school teacher's honey pot."

훈장님 is a polite way to refer to a 훈장 – a teacher at a village school for learning how to read and write Chinese.

훈장 = "(village school) teacher"

꿀단지 = "honey pot," "jar of honey"

옛날 옛적 작은 마을에 훈장님이 한 명 살고 있었습니다.

"Once upon a time in a small town lived a village school teacher."

옛날 옛적(에) = "long, long ago," "once upon a time"

훈장님의 꿀단지

그 훈장님은 아이들이 열심히 책을 읽고 있을 때 아이들 몰래 꿀을 꺼내서 먹곤 했습니다.

"When the children were diligently reading books, the teacher used to secretly take out honey and eat it."

몰래 is an adverb form of 모르다 ("to not know"), and means something is done in secret without anyone knowing about it. Here, 아이들 몰래 means "without the children knowing."

The ~곤 하다 grammar form is attached directly to an action verb stem and means that something happens frequently or regularly. It is most often used in the past tense to mean that someone "used to" frequently do something. ~곤 하다 is a more common shortened version of ~고는 하다.

몰래 = "secretly," "without anyone knowing"
~곤 하다 = "to do frequently," "to do regularly"

눈치가 빠른 아이 하나가 그 모습을 발견하고 훈장님에게 물었습니다.

"One quick-witted child discovered him, and asked the teacher."

눈치 is being able to recognize someone else's feelings, or the ability to read a situation. If someone has 빠른 눈치 ("fast wits") then they're able to quickly know what's going on around them, and to read what other people might be thinking or feeling.

모습 ("figure," "image") is often used to mean the "figure or image of (someone doing something)." So 그 모습 is referring to seeing the teacher secretly eating the honey, and you can think of it as meaning "what the teacher looked like when he was eating the honey."

Typically the verb 물어보다 is used to say "to ask," but it originally comes from 묻다 ("to ask") and 보다, meaning "to try asking" or literally "to ask and see how it goes." Although 물어보다 is used more often, 묻다 can be used when asking someone a direct question – not when you're simply curious about something.

눈치 = "wits," "senses"
눈치(가) 빠르다 = "to be quick-witted"
모습 = "figure," "image"
묻다 = "to ask"

"훈장님 저희에게는 엿가락 하나도 나눠 먹으라고 가르치시고 혼자 꿀을 드십니까?"

"Teacher, you teach us to share even one stick of taffy, and you're eating honey alone?"

엿가락 is a traditional snack, which is a small stick of taffy.

드시다 is the honorific verb form of 먹다 ("to eat").

저희 = "us," "we" (humble)
엿가락 = "stick of taffy"
나눠 먹다 = "to share (eating)"
드시다 = 먹다 (honorific)

그 말을 들은 훈장님은 "이건 꿀이 아니라 약이다. 아이들은 먹으면 죽는 약이야." 라고 거짓말을 했습니다.
"The teacher who heard that lied saying, 'This isn't honey, it's medicine. It's medicine that if children eat it they'll die.'"

아니라 (from the verb 아니다) can be used after a noun to mean "it's not (noun), but…." The Subject Marker (이/가) is most often attached to the noun. 아니라 is then followed by what the noun is instead. 꿀이 아니라 약이다 means "It's not honey, (but) it's medicine."

Note how the quoting form (here, the ~고 form) can be used with a large variety of verbs – not just 말(을) 하다. In the sentence here it's being used with 거짓말(을) 하다 meaning "to lie."

아니라 = "it's not (noun), but…"
약 = "medicine," "drug"
거짓말 = "lie," "falsehood"
거짓말(을) 하다 = "to lie"

하루는 훈장님이 아이들에게 책을 읽도록 시키고 잠시 외출을 했습니다.
"One day the teacher made the children read books, and went outside for a moment."

읽도록 means "so that (someone) reads," and adding 시키다 ("to make do," "to force") means that the teacher "made it" so that the children read. The person or people who are made to do something with this form are marked with the particle 에게 ("to").

~도록 시키다 = "to make (someone do)," "to force (someone to do)"
잠시 = "for a moment," "briefly"

"우리 꿀 한입씩만 먹을까?" 라고 한 아이가 말했습니다.
"'Should we each eat just a bite of honey?' one child said."

한입 literally means "one mouth." 입 ("mouth") can also be used as a counter for a bite or mouthful of something.

입 = bite or mouthful counter
한입 = "a bite," "a mouthful"

훈장님의 꿀단지

아이들이 한입씩 꿀을 먹다 보니 꿀단지는 금세 텅 비고 말았습니다.

"After the children each ate a bite of honey, they soon realized that the honey pot ended up completely empty."

먹다 보니 is a combination of 먹다 ("to eat") with 보다 ("to see"). Using an action verb in this way with 보다 shows that someone realizes something (literally, "sees" something) while doing that verb. Therefore, 먹다 보니 means "while eating, (someone) realized...." Using 보니 is common in writing, while 보니까 is more common in speaking.

금세 is a more common and shortened version of 금시에.

The ~고 말다 grammar form (used in 텅 비고 말았습니다) is typically only used in the past tense when explaining to someone else that something ended up happening – here in the sentence it means "it ended up (being) completely empty." This form is also only used when what happened was unintentional; it's not used to say that you ended up doing something that you intended to do (for that, use the much more common ~게 되다 grammar form instead.)

~다 보니(까) = "realizing something while (doing)"
금세 = "shortly," "soon," "immediately"
텅 비다 = "to be completely empty"
~고 말다 = "to end up (doing unintentionally)"
~게 되다 = "to end up (doing)"

훈장님에게 혼이 날 생각을 하니 아이들은 걱정이 되었습니다.

"The children became worried because they thought that they would be scolded by the teacher."

훈장님에게 here means "by the teacher." When using a passive verb, the particle 에게 ("by") can mark the person (or people) doing that verb – here, scolding the children. When something is instead done "by" an inanimate object, use the particle 에.

~에게 = "by (someone passively)"
~에 = "by (something passively)"
혼(이) 나다 = "to get in trouble," "to be scolded"

그때 똑똑한 아이 하나가 다른 아이들에게 바닥에 누워 있으라고 말하고 훈장님이 아끼는 벼루를 마당에 던져 깨뜨렸습니다.

"Then one smart child told the other children to lie down on the floor, and threw the teacher's cherished inkstone into the front yard, breaking it."

벼루 is an inkstone used for calligraphy. As the quality of an ink can affect the quality of calligraphy, some inkstones can be very expensive, as was likely the teacher's inkstone in this story.

훈장님의 꿀단지

깨뜨리다 is a stronger sounding version of the regular verb 깨다, meaning "to break (something)." 던져 깨뜨리다, which uses the verb 던지다 ("to throw"), literally means "to throw and break" or "to break by throwing."

그때 = "then," "that time"
아끼다 = "to save (by not using)," "to cherish"
벼루 = "inkstone"
마당 = "(front) yard"
던지다 = "to throw"
깨뜨리다 = "to break," "to smash," "to destroy"
깨다 = "to break," "to smash"

훈장님의 기침 소리가 들리기 시작하자 똑똑한 아이가 마당에 앉아 울기 시작했습니다.

"As soon as they started to hear the sound of the teacher coughing, the smart child sat down in the front yard and began to cry."

The ~자 ending (here as 시작하자) can also have the same meaning as the longer ~자마자 ending, meaning "as soon as."

기침 = "cough"
~자 = "as soon as"

놀라서 달려온 훈장님은 울고 있는 아이 옆에 깨진 벼루와 텅 빈 꿀단지를 보고 입을 다물 수가 없었습니다.

"The teacher, who came running because he was surprised, saw the broken inkstone and the completely empty honey pot next to the crying child and couldn't close his mouth."

달려오다 comes from 달리다 ("to run") and 오다 ("to come"), and means "to run (here)." The opposite is 달려가다, meaning "to run (somewhere else)."

입을 다물 수 없었습니다 means that the teacher's mouth was open in surprise, and that he couldn't shut it.

달리다 = "to run," "to dash"
달려오다 = "to come running," "to run (here)"
달려가다 = "to go running," "to run (somewhere else)"
깨지다 = "to be broken," "to be smashed"
입(을) 다물다 = "to shut (one's) mouth"

"훈장님 저희가 실수로 훈장님께서 아끼시는 벼루를 깼습니다."

"'Teacher, we accidentally broke your cherished inkstone."

실수로 = "by mistake," "by accident," "accidentally"

"그래서 훈장님의 약을 먹고 죽으려고 동무들과 약을 모두 먹었습니다."
"So we tried to eat your medicine to die, and ate all of the medicine with each other."

약을 먹고 죽으려고 uses the ~(으)려고 action verb ending (으려고 after a consonant or 려고 after a vowel) which shows intention – the children ate the medicine and intended to die (죽다). This form can then be followed by 하다 ("to do") or any other verb showing what someone does – here, it's used with 약(을) 먹다.

동무 is used in North Korea to mean "comrade," but it can also mean a friend or companion who's doing something together with you. Here, 동무들 means that they're all trying to eat the medicine to die together.

~(으)려고 = "intending to (do)"
약(을) 먹다 = "to take medicine" (literally, "to eat medicine")
동무 = "comrade," "friend," "companion"

그 이야기를 들은 훈장님은 아이들을 차마 혼내지 못하고 집으로 돌려보냈습니다.
"The teacher who heard that didn't have the heart to get mad at the children, and sent them back home."

차마 is an adverb that's used before a verb meaning "cannot" (such as before the ~수 없다 ending or 못하다). It means that someone is unable to do something, or that someone doesn't have the heart to do something.

차마 = "unable to," "not have the heart to"
혼(을) 내다 = "to get mad at," "to scold"
돌려보내다 = "to send back," "to return"

그 뒤에 훈장님은 아이들에게 거짓말을 한 것을 사과하고 아이들 몰래 꿀을 먹던 버릇을 고쳤다고 합니다.
"Afterwards the teacher apologized for having lied to the children, and fixed his (bad) habit of eating honey in secret."

버릇 means "habit," but is typically used for a bad habit. To say that something is a regular or good habit, use 습관 ("habit," "custom") instead.

꿀을 먹던 버릇 means "(bad) habit of eating honey." Here, the ~던 ending combined with an action verb shows that it used to happen in the past – literally, "the bad habit that the teacher used to eat honey."

그 뒤에 = "afterwards," "after (that)"
사과(를) 하다 = "to apologize"
버릇 = "(bad) habit"
습관 = "habit," "custom"

Glossary

ㄱ

가는 날이 장날이다 "to be bad (or good) timing," "as luck would have it"	#6
가려지다 "to be hidden," "to be covered"	#5
가리다 "to hide," "to cover"	#5
가정 "family," "household"	#9
각 "each" (prefix)	#7
각별하다 "to be particular," "to be special"	#8
~간 "for," "during" (after counter)	#7
갈아입다 "to change (clothing)"	#4
감성 "sense," "sensitivity"	#17
강수량 "rainfall (amount)"	#8
강아지 "puppy," "dog"	#14
개점 "opening (of a store)"	#7
개최(를) 하다 "to hold (a meeting or event)"	#9
거주 "residence"	#10
거주 국가 "country of residence"	#10
거짓말 "lie," "falsehood"	#21
거짓말(을) 하다 "to lie"	#21
걱정 "worry," "concern"	#20
걱정(을) 하다 "to worry," "to concern"	#4
걱정(이) 되다 "to become a worry," "to grow uneasy"	#20
걱정이다 "to be a worry," "to be worried about"	#20
건 "case," "matter"	#11
건설 "construction"	#9
건설(이) 되다 "to be constructed"	#9
걸어가다 "to walk (to somewhere)"	#4
~게 되다 "to end up (doing)"	#21
겨우 "(just) barely"	#4
겨울 바다 "winter sea"	#6
결국 "in the end," "ultimately"	#19
결정(을) 하다 "to decide"	#4
~고 나니(까) "and then," "after (doing)" (unexpectedly)	#19
~고 나서 "and then," "after (doing)"	#5
~고 말다 "to end up (doing unintentionally)"	#21
고르다 "to choose"	#4
고민(을) 하다 "to be concerned," "to (slightly) worry"	#4
~고서 ~고 나서	#5
~곤 하다 "to do frequently," "to do regularly"	#21
곧장 "right (away)," "straight"	#20
골프(를) 치다 "to play golf"	#17
곳곳 "various places," "all around (here and there)"	#9
공인 "official approval"	#11
공헌 "contribution"	#9
과연 "really," "indeed"	#5
과제 "assignment"	#12
관계자 "person(s) concerned," "person(s) connected," "official"	#9
관상 "fortune"	#19
교수 "professor"	#12
교수님 "professor" (title)	#12
구 "district (of a city)"	#5
구경(을) 하다 "to look around," "to see"	#5
~구나 (realizing something)	#5
구하다 "to rescue," "to save"	#2
국가 "nation," "country"	#10
국내 "domestic"	#7
군데 "place," "spot," place counter	#5
권고(를) 하다 "to advise," "to urge," "to recommend"	#8
규칙 "rule(s)," "regulation"	#10
그 뒤로 "afterward," "since then"	#19
그 뒤에 "afterwards," "after (that)"	#21
그 와중에 "meanwhile," "in the meantime"	#6
그대로 "(just/exactly) as it is"	#7
그때 "then," "that time"	#21
그래도 "(but) still," "however"	#15
그러고 나니(까) "after (doing) that," "next" (unexpectedly)	#19
그러고 나서 "after (doing) that," "next"	#5
그러다 "to say so," "to do so"	#2
그러다가 "and then (one day)"	#19
그림(을) 그리다 "to draw (a drawing)," "to paint (a picture)"	#17
금번 "this (time)," "this occasion"	#11
금세 "shortly," "soon," "immediately"	#21
급식 "(provided) meal," "meal service"	#9
~기 전에 "before doing"	#4
기관 "organization"	#11
기다랗다 "to be (very) long"	#16
기대(가) 되다 "to be expected"	#7

Glossary

~기도 하다 "to even (verb)" #9

~기로 하다 "to decide to do…" #4

~기(를) 바라다 "to hope (that)," "to wish (that)" #7

기린 "giraffe" #16

기상청 "National Weather Service," "weather center" #8

기숙사 "dormitory" #6

기숙사방 "dormitory room" #6

기술 "technology," "skill" #11

기억에 남다 "to remain in (one's) memory," "to be memorable" #6

기업 "company," "business" #7

~기에 "(in order) to" #11

기온 "(weather) temperature" #8

기자 "(news) reporter" #7

기재(를) 하다 "to write in," "to fill in" #10

기침 "cough" #21

~길 ~기를 #7

김 "dried seaweed," "(dried) laver" #1

깊이 "deeply," "in depth" #12

~까지 "(up) until," "(all the way) to (a location)" #4

~까지 "even (as much as)," "to go as far as to do" #4

깜빡 "with a flash" #3

깜빡 잠(이) 들다 "to fall asleep (without being aware of it)" #3

깜빡하다 "to forget (momentarily)" #1

깜짝 놀라다 "to be startled," "to be very surprised" #20

깨다 "to break," "to smash" #21

깨뜨리다 "to break," "to smash," "to destroy" #21

깨지다 "to be broken," "to be smashed" #21

꺼내다 "to take out," "to pull out" #4

껌 "gum" #6

껌이다 "to be a piece of cake" #6

꼬치 "(food on a) skewer" #4

~께 "to" (honorific) #4

~께서 Subject Marker (이/가) (honorific) #4

~께서는 Topic Marker (은/는) (honorific) #4

꿀단지 "honey pot," "jar of honey" #21

끈적하다 "to be slimy," "to be sticky" #16

끌고 가다 "to drag (along) somewhere" #6

끌다 "to pull," "to drag (along)" #6

끝에 "at the end," "at the close" #7

ㄴ

~나 보다 "to guess that," "something seems like" #17

~나 싶다 "to wonder (to oneself) if" #5

나누다 "to share," "to distribute" #9

나눠 먹다 "to share (eating)" #21

나타나다 "to appear," "to show up" #20

날다 "to fly" #3

남다 "to be left," "to remain" #2

남부 지방 "southern region" #8

낫다 "to recover," "to heal" #19

낮 기온 "daytime temperature" #8

내 정신 좀 봐. "I can't believe I've forgotten that." #1

내리다 "to get off (a vehicle)," "to disembark" #3

내용 "contents" #7

넉넉하다 "to be sufficient," "to be plenty," "to be enough" #18

네모(가) 나다 "to be square (shaped)" #13

넥타이 "(neck)tie" #1

넷이서 "the four of," "together (as four)" #5

노부부 "elderly couple," "old couple" #20

노숙인 "homeless (person)" #9

노숙인 쉼터 "homeless shelter" #9

노인 "elderly," "senior citizen" #9

놀다 "to play," "to hang out" #6

놀라다 "to be surprised," "to be amazed" #20

놀이공원 "amusement park" #7

놀이기구 "(amusement) ride" #7

놓고 가다 "to forget to take," "to leave (something) and go" #1

놓고 오다 "to forget to bring," "to leave (something) and come" #1

누락 "omission," "leaving out" #12

누락(이) 되다 "to be omitted," "to be left out," "to be missing" #12

눈 맞춤 "eye contact" #16

눈치 "wits," "senses" #21

눈치(가) 빠르다 "to be quick-witted" #21

눈치(를) 채다 "to notice," "to sense" #20

느껴지다 "to be felt," "to feel" #20

Glossary

~느라고 "because," "due to" (negative outcome)	#6
~는 것(을) "that (verb)," "the fact that (verb)"	#19
~니 (showing curiosity, casual)	#17
님 formal title ending	#11
ㄷ	
~다 보니(까) "realizing something while (doing)"	#21
다국적 "multinational"	#7
다녀오다 "to go and come back"	#1
~다니 (showing an emotional reaction)	#5
다들 "everybody," "everyone"	#6
다람쥐 "squirrel"	#14
다시 한번 "once more," "(once) again," "a second time"	#12
다양하다 "to be diverse," "to be various/varied"	#9
다행 "good fortune," "luck"	#4
단단하다 "to be solid," "to be firm"	#13
달려가다 "to go running," "to run (somewhere else)"	#21
달려오다 "to come running," "to run (here)"	#21
달리다 "to run," "to dash"	#21
담당자 "person in charge"	#10
담백하다 "to be light," "to be bland"	#13
답답하다 "to be frustrated," "to be irritated," "to feel (emotionally) heavy"	#19
당나귀 "donkey"	#19
당당하다 "to be confident," "to be dignified," "to be proud"	#19
당분간 "for some time," "for the time being"	#4
당시 "at that time"	#9
당신 "darling," "you"	#1
대 generation counter	#7
대기업 "large corporation," "conglomerate"	#7
대나무 "bamboo"	#19
대충 "approximately," "roughly," "of sorts," "sloppily," "without care"	#5
대통령 "president"	#2
대통령 상 "Presidential Award"	#9
대형 "large size"	#7
대회 "competition," "tournament"	#10
댓글 "(social media) comment"	#16
~더라 (personally experienced, casual)	#4
~더라고(요) (personally experienced)	#4
더불어 "together (with)," "along (with)"	#9
~던 (repeatedly used to happen)	#5
~던가 "whether it was (I don't know)..."	#6
던지다 "to throw"	#21
덤 "freebie," "extra (thing)"	#16
~데 "(in order) to"	#7
데 "place"	#7
~데도 "even though"	#4
데이터 "data"	#11
데이트(를) 하다 "to (go on a) date"	#5
도 degree counter	#8
도끼 "axe"	#20
~도록 "so that," "in order to"	#8
~도록 시키다 "to make (someone do)," "to force (someone to do)"	#21
도루묵 "sailfin sandfish"	#6
도시락 "lunch box," "prepared (box) lunch"	#1
도움(을) 받다 "to get/receive help"	#4
도움(이) 되다 "to be helpful"	#7
도착시간 "arrival time"	#3
독거 "living alone," "solitary life"	#9
독거노인 "senior citizen living alone"	#9
돌려보내다 "to send back," "to return"	#21
돌보다 "to take care of," "to look after"	#20
동 "neighborhood (in a district)"	#5
동무 "comrade," "friend," "companion"	#21
동물원 "zoo"	#16
동아리 "club," "group"	#9
동의(를) 하다 "to agree," "to consent"	#10
동해 "East Sea"	#6
두부 "tofu"	#13
둘러보다 "to (have a) look around," "to browse"	#4
둘이 "two people," "the two of us/them"	#4
둘이서 "the two of," "together (as two)"	#5
뒤 "after," "behind"	#2
드디어 "finally," "at last"	#2
드라마 "drama (show)"	#5
드르렁 (드르렁) (sound of snoring)	#3
드리다 "to give" (humble)	#4
드림 "from" (formal)	#11
드시다 먹다 (honorific)	#21
들려오다 "to be heard (here)," "to reach (one's) ears"	#19

Glossary

들르다 "to stop by" #4

들어가다 "to enter (in)" #4

들여다보다 "to look in(to)" #20

듬뿍 "full," "heaping" "generously" #18

~듯 "(seems) as if," "(seems) as though" #18

등 "and so on," "and others," "etc." #9

등으로 "and such," "et cetera," "and so on" #8

따라가다 "to (go) follow" #20

따라오다 "to (come) follow" #20

따르다 "to follow" #6

따르릉 (따르릉) ring (sound of telephone, bicycle bell, alarm clock) #2

딱 "just (exactly)," "perfectly" #6

떡볶이 "spicy rice cakes" #4

또 한 번 "once (more) again" #9

또한 "also," "in addition" #10

똑같이 "identically," "(just) like," "the same" #6

뚱뚱하다 "to be fat," "to be plump" #13

뜨다 "to scoop (up)," "to scoop (out)" #20

ㄹ

로 "road," "street" #11

ㅁ

마다 "each" (suffix) #7

마당 "(front) yard" #21

마땅하다 "to be right," "to be appropriate" #4

마을 "village," "town" #20

마음에 들다 "to like" #4

만족 "satisfaction" #17

~만큼 "as much as," "amount" #17

말 "end (part)" #9

맛집 "good place (for food)," "popular store" #18

매달 "every month" #9

매출 "sales" #11

매출표 "sales statement" #11

맴돌다 "to circle (an area)" #20

먹이 "(animal) food," "feed" #16

먼바다 "out at sea," "offshore" #8

먼저 "first" (adverb) #10

멀쩡하다 "to be fine," "to be okay," "to be unhurt" #20

메아리 "echo" #19

메이크업(을) 하다 "to put on makeup," "to wear makeup" #5

메주 "block of dried fermented soybeans" #6

며칠째 "for a few days," "for the past few days" #8

모 (tofu) block counter #13

모두 "all," "everyone," "everything" #19

모습 "figure," "image" #21

모으다 "to gather," "to save up (money)" #5

목걸이 "necklace" #5

목(이) 마르다 "to be thirsty" #20

몰래 "secretly," "without anyone knowing" #21

몸살 "(whole body) sickness (from exhaustion)" #17

몸살(이) 나다 "to get sick (from exhaustion)" #17

무릎 "knee," "lap" #20

무역학과 "international trade (major)" #12

무작정 "without any plan," "thoughtlessly," "randomly" #6

묻다 "to ask" #21

물감 "paint (for painting)" #17

물결 "tide," "flow" #8

뭐 "(so) whatever," "anyway" #5

미모 "(one's) beauty," "pretty face," "pretty looks," "pretty features" #5

미술 "art," "fine art," "painting," "drawing" #17

미인 "beauty," "beautiful person" #16

밀떡 "wheat flour cakes" #5

및 "and" #9

ㅂ

바라다 "to hope," "to wish" #7

바람에 "due to (something negative)" #4

바르다 "to apply," "to spread" #4

박사 "doctor (Ph.D.)" #7

발견(을) 하다 "to discover," "to spot" #20

발바닥 "palm," "paw" #8

발생(을) 하다 "to occur," "to happen" #8

밤(을) 새우다 "to stay up all night" #6

밤(이) 오다 "night comes" #15

배경 "background" #7

배우 "actor" #5

배추 "cabbage" #3

백성 "the people," "the public" #19

버릇 "(bad) habit" #21

벗어나다 "to get out (of)," "to break away (from)" #7

베다 "to chop," "to cut" #19

벼루 "inkstone" #21

Glossary

변신(을) 하다 "to transform," "to change" #2

병 "disease," "illness" #19

보관(이) 되다 "to be kept," "to be stored" #10

본(을) 뜨다 "to copy (something)," "to be modeled after (something)" #7

본격적 "regular," "real," "full-fledged" #11

본격적으로 "in earnest," "for real," "full-scale" #11

봉사 "service," "work" #9

봉사 활동 "service project," "volunteer work" #9

뵈다 "to see" (humble) #12

뵙다 "to see" (extra humble) #12

부끄러움 "embarrassment," "shame" #19

부부 "(married) couple," "husband and wife" #20

부상 "additional prize (item)" #10

부족하다 "to be insufficient," "to be lacking" #4

부탁(을) 드리다 부탁(을) 하다 (humble) #11

부탁(을) 하다 "to request," "to ask for" #11

북부 지방 "northern region" #8

북상(을) 하다 "to go north," "to move north" #8

분명 "certainly," "clearly," "obviously" #6

분명히 "clearly," "certainly," "plainly," "definitely" #6

불행 "misfortune" #4

비(가) 내리다 "to rain" #8

비결 "secret (method)" #20

비치다 "to shine" #5

비행기 표 "plane ticket" #10

빈칸 "blank(s)," "blank space" #10

~뿐이다 "all it is, is...," "it's just..." #6

ㅅ

사과(를) 하다 "to apologize" #21

사내 "in-house," "in the company" #9

사이 "between" #7

사이 "space (between)" #20

사이에서 "among (noun)" #7

사회 "society," "community" #9

사회 공헌 "social contribution" #9

산속 "far up in a mountain" #14

상 "prize," "award" #9

상상력 "imagination" #7

새 "new" #11

새끼 "child" (informal) #14

샘물 "spring water" #20

생각(이) 나다 "to think of," "something comes to mind," "to be remembered" #4

생기다 "to occur," "to be formed" #20

생년월일 "(full) birthdate" #10

생신 "birthday" (honorific) #4

서랍 "drawer" #4

서울시 "the city of Seoul" #9

서점 "bookstore" #7

성군 "great and wise king" #19

성별 "gender," "sex" #10

세상(을) 구하다 "to save the world" #2

세상에서 "in the world" #15

셋이서 "the three of," "together (as three)" #5

소문 "rumor," "gossip" #19

소스 "sauce" #18

속 "(deep) inside" #7

속눈썹 "eyelash(es)" #16

속도 "speed," "velocity" #8

손 편지 "handwritten letter" #4

수강(을) 하다 "to take a course," "to take a class" #6

수상(을) 하다 "to be awarded," "to receive (a prize)" #9

수업 "class," "lesson" (taught by a teacher) #4

숲 "forest," "grove" #19

쉼터 "rest area," "shelter" #9

슝 "whoosh" (sound of wind, flying) #3

습관 "habit," "custom" #21

시간(이) 지나다 "time passes," "time goes by" #20

시름시름 앓다 "to suffer (from an illness) for a long time" #19

시외 "outside the city," "countryside" #6

시원하다 "to be cool," "to be refreshing" #13

시장님 "(city) mayor" #2

신기하다 "to be awesome," "to be amazing" #5

신중하다 "to be cautious," "to be careful" #4

실물 "real (thing, person)," "genuine (thing, person)" #5

실수로 "by mistake," "by accident," "accidentally" #21

십 대 "teenagers" #7

쌀떡 "rice flour cakes" #5

쑤다 "to cook grains (by boiling)" #6

씀 "from" (informal) #11

~씩 "each," "a," "per" #9

Glossary

ㅇ

~(아/어/etc.) 보이다 "to look (descriptive verb)" #4
~(아/어/etc.) 서 그런지 "whether it's because...," "maybe it's because..." #4
~(아/어/etc.) 하다 "to feel (descriptive verb)" #5
~(아/어/etc.) 하다 3rd person verbs (wants, desires, emotions) #4
아끼다 "to save (by not using)," "to cherish" #21
아니면 "or" #2
아래 "the bottom," "below," "under" #10
아르바이트 "part-time job" #4
아르바이트생 "a student working a part-time job" #4
아무거나 "whatever," "anything" #5
아무래도 "anyway," "either way" #5
아우우우 howling (onomatopoeia) #14
아차! "Oh my!," "Darn it!," "My goodness!" #1
아티스트 "artist" #17
악당 "villain," "bad guy" #2
알려드리다 알려주다 (humble) #10
알려주다 "to tell," "to let (someone) know" #10
알려지다 "to be (well) known" #9
알리다 "to let (someone) know," "to tell," "to inform" #19
알바 "part-time job" #4
앓다 "to suffer (from an illness)" #19
앞서 "previously (before now)," "beforehand," "ahead (of)," "earlier" #10
앞으로 "from now (on)," "in the future" #6
액세서리 "accessory" #5
~야지 "better," "gotta," "have to" #4
약속시간 "appointment/meeting time" #4
아니라 "it's not (noun), but..." #21
약화 "weakening" #8
약 "medicine," "drug" #21
약(을) 먹다 "to take medicine" (literally, "to eat medicine") #21
어느 "a (certain)," "some" #19
어머 (어머)! "Oh my!" #2
어묵 "fish cake" #4
억지로 "against one's will," "by force," "forcefully" #6
얼마나 "how (much)," "how" #3
엄청 "very," "terribly," "seriously," "awfully" #6
엄청나다 "to be tremendous," "to be incredible" #19
~에 "by (something passively)" #21
~에 늦다 "to be late to" #4
~에게 "by (someone passively)" #21
여러 "a number of," "several," "many" #4
여러 곳 "a number of places," "several places" #4
여보 "honey," "sweetheart" #1
여전히 "as usual," "as ever," "still" #19
역시 "as (one) expected," "as (one) knew," "of course" #5
연상(을) 하게 하다 "to remind" #7
연상(을) 하다 "to be reminiscent of something" #7
연애(를) 하다 "to have a romantic relationship," "to go out with (someone)" #6
연예인 "celebrity," "performer" #5
연탄 "(coal) briquette" #9
열심히 듣다 "to be all ears," "to listen intently" #19
엿가락 "stick of taffy" #21
영향 "influence," "effect" #8
옆집 "next door (house)," "neighbor (house)" #14
예상 "expectation," "prediction," "forecast" #8
예상(을) 하다 "to expect," "to forecast," "to predict" #8
예상(이) 되다 "to be expected," "to be forecasted," "to be predicted" #8
예술 "art (in general)" #17
예전 "the past," "a long time ago" #17
옛날 "the old days" #17
옛날 옛적(에) "long, long ago," "once upon a time" #21
오도도도 something small running quickly (mimetic word) #14
오래오래 "forever," "for a very long time" #19
오랜만에 "after a long time," "(for the first time) in a long time" #5
오르다 "to go up," "to rise," "to increase" #3
오른쪽 "right (side)" #3
오븐 "oven" #18
온도 "(object) temperature" #8
올리다 "to raise," "to increase" #3
올림 "from" (extra formal) #11
~(와/과) 함께 "together with..." #4
와다다다 something large running quickly (mimetic word) #14
왕복 "round-trip" #10
외출 "going out(side)" #8

Glossary

외출(을) 하다 "to go out(side)" #8

외치다 "to shout," "to exclaim" #19

왼쪽 "left (side)" #3

요청(을) 드리다 요청(을) 하다 (humble) #11

요청(을) 하다 "to request," "to ask for" #11

욕심 "greed" #20

욕심쟁이 "greedy person" #20

우끼끼끼 primate shout (onomatopoeia) #14

우리나라 "Korea" (literally, "our country") #8

우편 번호 "zip code," "postal code" #11

울 집 "our house," "my house" (우리 집) #14

원래 "originally," "always (from the beginning)" #6

유치원 "preschool" #7

~(으)니 ~(으)니까 #4

~(으)려고 "intending to (do)" #21

(으)로 인하다 "to be due to," "to be as a result of" #8

~(으)며 "while," "and" #4

~(으)면 좋겠다 "I hope...," "I wish..." #4

~(으)면서 "while doing" #4

으악 "Ugh!," "Ah!" (surprise) #3

~(은/는)커녕 "let alone...," "rather than...," "forget..." #6

~(을/ㄹ) 겸 (two actions for the same purpose) #4

~(을/ㄹ) 기세이다 "to look/appear like someone will do," "to be ready to do" #4

~(을/ㄹ) 뻔하다 "to almost (do)," "to nearly (do)" #1

~(을/ㄹ) 수밖에 없다 "nothing one can do but" #4

~(을/를) 통해(서) "through," "by way of" #9

~의 영향으로 "due to...," "as a result of" #8

의성어 "onomatopoeia" #14

의태어 "mimetic word" #14

이 외에(도) "in addition (to this/that)" #9

~(이)가 "from" (casual) #11

이것저것 "this and that" #4

~(이)나 "or something," "no less than," "as much/long as," "as many as," "about" #4

이달 "this month" #9

이달 말 "the end of this month" #9

이달 초 "the beginning of this month" #9

이래서 "therefore," "so" #6

이런 "darn," "dang it" #1

이루다 "to make," "to attain," "to fulfill" #19

이메일 주소 "email address" #10

이목 "attention" #7

이목(을) 끌다 "to attract attention" #7

~(이)자 "and" (for connecting states) #7

인기몰이 "gaining popularity," "becoming a hit" #5

인생 "(human) life" #6

인증서 "certificate (of authentication)" #11

일깨우다 "to awaken," "to enlighten" #7

일다 "to rise (wind, water)" #8

일부 지역 "some areas," "some regions" #8

~일뿐이다 "all it is, is...," "it's just..." (negative meaning) #6

일어나다 "to stand up," "to get up" #20

임금 "king," "ruler" #19

임금님 "king," "ruler" (honorific) #19

임직원 "staff (member)," "employee" #9

입 bite or mouthful counter #21

입(을) 다물다 "to shut (one's) mouth" #21

입맛 "(one's) taste," "(one's) palate" #5

입상(을) 하다 "to win (a reward)" #10

ㅈ

~자 "as soon as" #21

자극 "stimulus," "stimulation" #7

자기 "oneself" #19

자라다 "to grow (up)," "to be raised" #20

~자마자 "as soon as" #18

자발적 "voluntary" #9

자발적으로 "voluntarily" #9

자발적이다 "to be voluntary" #9

자식 "child(ren)," "offspring" #20

자신 "oneself" #19

자신의 "one's own" #19

자제(를) 하다 "to refrain from (verb)" #8

잔뜩 "to one's fill," "filled" #20

잘 "well," "often" #19

잠 "sleep" #15

잠그다 "to lock" #2

잠시 "for a moment," "briefly" #21

장 flat object counter #9

장인 "(master) artisan," "(skilled) craftsman" #19

저녁으로 "for dinner" #4

저소득 "low-income" #9

저소득 가정 "low-income family" #9

저희 "us," "we" (humble) #21

Glossary

적극적이다 "to be active and positive" #9

전 "every," "all" #9

전국 "whole country," "whole nation" #8

전국적으로 "nationally," "nationwide," "all over the (whole) country" #8

~전까지 "before (and not after)" #10

전달 "delivery (of something)," "conveying (information)" #9

전달(을) 하다 "to deliver (something)," "to convey (information)" #9

전래 동화 "traditional folk tale" #19

전망(을) 하다 "to forecast," "to foresee," "to predict" #8

전화 "phone call" #2

전화번호 "(tele)phone number" #10

젊다 "to be young," "to be youthful" #20

점수 "grade," "score" #12

점쟁이 "fortune-teller" #19

정글 "jungle" #14

정기적이다 "to be regular," "to be periodic" #9

정성스럽다 "to be sincere," "to be careful and respectful" #20

제출(을) 하다 "to submit," "to turn in" #12

조르다 "to nag," "to pester" #20

좋아요 "(social media) like" #16

주위 "surrounding (area)," "around (somewhere)" #20

주의 "care," "caution" #8

죽을병 "fatal disease," "terminal illness" #19

준비(가) 되다 "to be prepared" #7

~줄(을) 알다 "to think (that)," "to know (that)," "to expect (that)" #6

중간 "middle," "between," "midterm" #12

중부 지방 "central region" #8

중이다 "to be in the middle of doing" #5

증진(을) 시키다 "to enhance," "to increase" #7

~지 모르겠다 "to not know whether/if..." #4

~지 못하다 "unable to (do)," "can't (do)" #4

~지... ~지 "whether (or not)" #4

지나다 "to pass," "to go by" #20

지내다 "to associate with," "to get along with" #4

~지다 "to become (descriptive verb)" #17

지반 "ground (surface)" #8

지속(이) 되다 "to continue," "to persist" #8

지속적으로 "continuously," "consistently" #9

~지요 ~죠 #19

지우다 "to wipe off," "to erase" #4

직접 "directly," "personally" #4

진리 "truth," "the best" #6

진심으로 "sincerely," "from the (bottom of someone's) heart" #10

진행 "progress" #11

진행(을) 하다 "to progress," "to preside over," "to carry on" #11

진행(이) 되다 "to progress," "to go along" #9

집 "house," "home," "place (restaurant)" #18

~짜리 "worth (of)," "amount (of)" #7

ㅊ

차마 "unable to," "not have the heart to" #21

착하다 "to be good-natured," "to be kindhearted" #20

참가 "participation," "entry" #10

참고로 "for reference," "for your information," "by the way" #10

참여(를) 하다 "to participate," "to take part in" #9

창립 "foundation," "establishment" #9

창립(이) 되다 "to be founded," "to be established" #9

창의력 "creativity" #7

찾다 "to look for," "to find," "to visit (somewhere)" #7

찾아가다 "to (go and) visit," "to drop by" #19

찾아보다 "to find," "to search for," "to go visit," "to pay (someone) a visit" #12

찾아오다 "to (come and) visit," "to drop by" #19

채널 "(TV, etc.) channel" #10

척하다 "to pretend," "to act" #16

첨부(를) 하다 "to attach (something)," "to add (something)" #10

첫째 주 "first week" #9

청소년 "adolescent," "youth" #7

체온 "(body) temperature" #8

체하다 "to pretend," "to act" #16

체험(을) 하다 "to experience (firsthand)" #7

초 "beginning (part)" #9

초등학교 저학년 "the first 1-3 years of elementary school" #7

최고 "maximum," "at most," "(the) best" #8

최근 "the latest," "the most recent" #11

최소 "minimum," "at least" #8

최우수상 "grand prize" #10

Glossary

최저 "minimum," "the lowest" #8

최종 "final," "last" #4

최종적으로 "finally," "lastly," "in the end" #4

최종적이다 "to be the final," "to be the last," "to be the definitive" #4

추가적 "additional" #10

추가적으로 "additionally" #10

추가적이다 "to be additional" #10

축구 "soccer" #15

축제날 "holiday," "festival day" #6

축하(를) 드리다 축하(를) 하다 (humble) #10

축하(를) 하다 "to congratulate" #10

출근(을) 하다 "to (leave to) go to work" #3

충격 "shock" #19

취미생활 "(life) having hobbies," "(life) enjoying hobbies" #17

층 (building) floor counter #7

침 "saliva," "spit" #16

침팬지 "chimpanzee" #14

칭송 "praise," "admiration" #19

ㅋ

커다랗다 "to be (very) big" #19

커플 "couple," "two people (in a relationship)" #5

컨설팅 "consulting" #11

~케 ~하게 #7

쿠킹 "cooking" #18

큰소리로 "out loud," "with a loud voice" #19

큰일 "problem," "trouble" (literally, "big issue") #1

큰일(이) 나다 "to be a big problem," "to get into trouble" #1

ㅌ

태어나서 처음 "(for) the first time ever in my life" #6

태평성대 "reign of peace" #19

태풍 "typhoon" #8

텅 비다 "to be completely empty" #21

테마 "theme" #7

토핑 "topping" #18

통 container counter #10

특히 "particularly," "especially" #5

팀장 "team leader" #11

ㅍ

파기(가) 되다 "to be destroyed," "to be shredded," "to be broken/cancelled" #10

파도 "(water) wave" #6

파이팅! "(Let's) go!" #10

팥 "red (adzuki) beans" #6

팥으로 메주(를) 쑨다 해도 믿겠다 "No matter what you say, (I) will believe you." #6

페인팅 "painting" #17

페퍼로니 "pepperoni" #18

편도 "one-way" #10

편지지 "stationary paper" #4

평가 "review," "rating" #7

평생 "(in) one's whole life" #5

평소 "usual," "ordinary" #20

평소처럼 "as usual," "as ordinary" #20

포대 "(burlap) bag," "sack" #9

포장(을) 하다 "to wrap up" #4

피망 "bell pepper" #18

피자집 "pizza parlor," "pizza restaurant" #18

피해 "damage," "harm" #8

필요하다 "to be necessary" #8

ㅎ

하기 "following," "under" #11

하여 해(서) #7

하늘(을) 날다 "to fly in the sky" #3

하루 "(one) day" #5

학기 "(school) semester" #6

학번 "student number" #12

학부모 "parents (or guardians) of students" #7

학점 "(school) credit" #6

한 몸 "one (body)" #6

한걸음에 "without stopping," "without (taking) a break" #20

한국행 "to(ward) Korea" #10

(한)복판 "the (very) center," "the heart (of somewhere)" #7

한입 "a bite," "a mouthful" #21

한참 동안 "for a long time," "for quite some time" #19

합치다 "to combine" #4

해상 "sea," "on the sea" #8

해안지역 "coastal area," "coastal region" #8

행사 "event," "ceremony" #9

허겁지겁 "in a rush," "hastily" #20

Glossary

헌혈 "blood donation"		#9
혼(을) 내다 "to get mad at," "to scold"		#21
혼(이) 나다 "to get in trouble," "to be scolded"		#21
화 episode counter		#1
화장품 "cosmetics"		#4
확인(을) 하다 "to check," "to confirm"		#12
활동 "activity"		#7
효녀 "obedient (devoted) daughter"		#20
효자 "obedient (devoted) son"		#20
후광 "(Buddhist) halo"		#5
후광(이) 비치다 "to have a halo"		#5
훈장 "(village school) teacher"		#21
힘(을) 얻다 "to take heart," "to be encouraged"		#19

Special Thanks

I want to give an extra "thank you" to the following supporters who have continually helped and supported me to create new content (such as this book). Each of you directly contributed to this book's creation.

Joel Tersigni
Courtney S
Kate Blais (이현주)
애슐리
KaitJoon | 김재화
Mikookoppa
Devon Smith
Guillermo Robles Wismann
Rodrigo Diaz
GirlNextDoor
Kristen Oliphant
Lauren Wilson
Lorrany Bastos
Gina Cianfoni
anonymomification
니카 (박수지)
Jeff Dallien
Clea B.
Anne Laymond
Arran Ireland
Daniela Salazar
smol
Mergik

Ben Vezzani
John Man
심태환
Ajedsshi
A-Huimang
Alli & Aubrey
Carrie Wrich
Margarita
Samantha Cashmore
Grandpamikee
Alexander "Harnik" Herbst
Jordi Kroon
Sarah Kitt
Tehila Gomez
Myles Dodge
Brenna Rae Smith
Irene Xandra Mae Lim
Austin Headrick
Kevin Fu
Starlit
Jessica Bridges
Kanani
Trevarr

손소현
Erian Stone
Sheka
Alison Hansel
Amaryliz - 보라
Celeste ♡
Cloud
Francesca Cavazzana
DefZen3
Calamityjane69
Marie Neer
NunyuhBusiness
Twice once
AerynSG
Sarah LeCrenier
Michał Majda
사라
this_neverworks
Sam Strongarm
Haley
Megan Chan
Madi Martinez
Laurence Jones

About the Author

Thank you for checking out my book! 감사합니다! I hope you enjoyed reading it as much as I enjoyed writing it. If you enjoyed this book, I'd love if you would leave a review at your favorite retailer. And keep an eye out for my future projects too. I'm always working hard creating new ways to help you learn Korean. Good luck in your studies!

About the Author:

Billy Go has been working as a Korean translator since 2008 with his B.A. in Korean, and currently teaches Korean online. He has spent several years living in South Korea, and still visits often.

Connect with me:

Subscribe to my videos on **YouTube**: youtube.com/gobillykorean
Follow me on **Twitter**: twitter.com/gobillykorean
Like me on **Facebook**: facebook.com/gobillykorean
Subscribe to my **Blog**: www.gobillykorean.com

Made in the USA
Las Vegas, NV
12 September 2024

95212186R00063